W9-CHO-761

Don't Be a Wife to a Boyfriend

10 Lessons I Learned When I Was Single

Shonda B. White

Don't Be a Wife to a Boyfriend

Copyright © June 2016 Shonda B. White

All rights reserved. No part of this publication may be reproduced, distributed, or transmitted in any form or by any means, including photocopying, recording, or other electronic or mechanical methods, without the prior written permission of the publisher, except in the case of brief quotations embodied in critical reviews and certain other noncommercial uses permitted by copyright law.

For more information, contact:

ShondaBrownWhite.com

ISBN-13: 978-1533066664

ISBN-10: 1533066663

Printed in the U.S.A.

AceStounding Publishing, first edition for print, June 2016

Dedication

I dedicate this book to the love of my life—my husband. Thank you for showing me real love still exists.

I also dedicate this book to all of my single and married sisters—those who, despite their single seasons, waiting periods, or past experiences, still believe in true love.

Contents

Introduction To My Single Journey   1

Lesson One:

Accept Self-Love Before You Accept Love From Someone Else   5

Lesson Two:

Let It Flow, But Don't Get Stuck In The Gray Area   23

Lesson Three:

Don't Think Of Him As A Piece Of Clay You Can Mold Into What You Want Him To Be   33

Lesson Four:

Don't Expect Different Results Using The Same Habits   45

Lesson Five:

Don't Confuse Love With Lust   59

Lesson Six:

Make Yourself A Priority While You Can   71

Lesson Seven:

Don't Make Excuses For People Who Need To Be Excused From Your Life   87

Lesson Eight:

Don't Be A Wife To A Boyfriend   105

Lesson Nine:

Don't Be That Girl: Over 30 And Worried   119

Lesson Ten:

Nothing Happens Overnight; Things Take Time   131

Introduction to my Single Journey

Hey, girlfriend!

Can I be real with you? Before you go on this journey with me, please hear me when I say this.

I can't tell you who to be.

I can't tell you whom to love.

I can't tell you if you'll ever meet "the one."

I can't tell you how or where to find true love.

I can't tell you how to feel or how long to feel it.

I can't tell you what the silver bullet is when it comes to love.

I can't tell you how long it's going to hurt or how many tears you'll shed.

All I can tell you is I've been hurt before.

All I can tell you is what worked for me.

All I can tell you is what I went through.

All I can tell you is that, at one point, I did give up on love.

All I can tell you is that you deserve nothing but the best.

All I can tell you is that I'm in love, but it didn't happen overnight.

All I can tell you is that I was young and dumb and made some mistakes.

All I can tell you is that sometimes things don't always go as planned.

All I can tell you is that I learned a lot along the way about life and love.

With that said...It's been almost eight years since I said, "I do," and approximately ten years since I first met the love of my life. Just so you know, my so-called fairy-tale ending didn't just happen. Before my married season, I had a single season. It was during my single season that I learned a lot about myself.

People see my marriage and assume it was easy, but it wasn't. Some people don't know what I went through prior to getting married. They don't understand my journey or even know how many mistakes I made along the way. They don't know about the hurt and betrayal and how I almost gave up on love and dating altogether. Even though I'm happily married now, there was a time when I would cry myself to sleep at night, wondering if and when it was going happen for me. I know I'm not the only one who's gone through that.

That's why I've always had a special place in my heart for my single sisters, because I've been there. Nowadays, it seems as if it's even harder than when I was single and dating.

Nevertheless, there is something about the journey of a woman and our shared experiences related to dating, love, and everything in between. We bond and heal through the experiences of each other. We encourage and remind each other that there's more to life than our relationship status. We realize others share similar experiences, so we no longer assume we're the only ones going through certain situations.

I get it. There are times when, over the course of our single seasons, we find ourselves stuck or torn between our hearts and minds. We go back and forth between settling and what we truly deserve. So, every now and then, we need a little pick-me-up and that, my dear sister, is what I'm here for.

One would assume, because I am married, that it's quite easy to say, "Don't worry. It'll be okay. You'll find someone." But I can't say that. I can't tell you how to feel, nor can I predict that you will experience true love in this lifetime, because God has a different plan for everyone.

While I do believe things fall into place as they should and what's meant to be will be, I come from a place of *I've been where you've been.* I've cried some of the same tears. I've held onto certain people and waited around for too long. I've been cheated on. I've been lied to. I've experienced betrayal, and, at one point, I was done with love...*but God!* Yes, there were times when I was an emotional wreck, but it's wonderful to know that one day I was able to look back on everything and declare, "I'm good," well before my husband came along.

Hence, it is my hope that the lessons I learned will encourage, inspire, and empower you, or someone else, to live with purpose and to live through the pain, while learning from my experiences and embracing the life God has for you regardless of your relationship status.

Lesson One

Accept self-love before you accept love from someone else.

I sat down on the bed timidly. I remember the room was what you would expect of a typical parent's room with a nice large bed, dresser, mirror, and chest. I vaguely remember the comforter spread across the bed. I think the fabric was a floral pattern in vibrant colors of pink and green. I was so nervous. My heart pounded so fast that I could literally hear it.

Every time I heard a noise, I jumped thinking someone was going to burst through the door and catch us. He started undressing me, but I mostly just lay there. It was like an out-of-body experience. He knew it was my first time, but it wasn't for him, so it made sense for him to take the lead. I was unsure if I really wanted to do it, but I didn't want to come off as scared. So, I just let it happen.

It started.

It happened.

We did it.

I was nearly fourteen years old when I lost my virginity.

Most girls my age were more concerned about slumber parties and school dances. That's not to say those things didn't matter to me as well, but I was more concerned with getting the attention from boys. So, there I was laying on a bed totally disconnected to what was taking place. I remember thinking to myself, "What on earth am I doing?" "What if my mom finds out?" She would have killed me…well, not really but you get my gist. Plus, I wasn't even allowed to have a boyfriend at the age of fourteen anyway.

I thought about what others would say and how disappointed everyone would be if they knew little miss "church girl" was having sex. Yes, I attended Sunday school every week, served on the usher board, sang in the choir, and even started directing the choir at a young age. I contemplated all of this during the sexual encounter, but it didn't compel me enough to stop.

We just kept going. Never once did I ask him to stop, because at the time that's what I thought I wanted. I had become so enthralled with what I heard around school. I wanted to fit in and I wanted him to like me, so I continued doing it anyway. If I was to be completely honest with myself, I can say not only did I want him to like me, but I actually wanted him to brag about me, so other guys would eventually be interested in me as well.

When it was all said and done, I felt numb. I felt conflicted. I felt guilty. I felt horrible. I don't even remember talking much about it with him once we finished. To this day, I barely remember all that took place during the sexual exchange. I couldn't tell you if it was good or bad, quite honestly (not that it matters), because both of us were way too young to understand the act of sexual intimacy. I just remember saying our goodbyes and that he said he would call me later. Then, I walked back home.

Fast forward to my late teens and early twenties.

When I was finally allowed to date during my high school years thereafter, I did whatever I could to have and maintain a serious relationship. Yes, at the ages of 16, 18, 19, and so on, I was more concerned with being committed and less concerned with having platonic relationships with guys. Stay with me, because I promise there's a reason why I'm telling you this.

> "Note to self: Self-esteem has everything to do with myself, not everyone else."

In college, I think I had a different boyfriend every year.

There was the one upperclassman whom I started dating during my naïve freshman year of college. I thought I was really doing something. I figured, since he was a few years older than me, that he would be ready to settle down much sooner than the younger guys I dated before.

Then, there was the other guy, who clearly wasn't ready to be in a committed relationship (neither was I now that I look back on it). I continued dating him off and on for two to three years, because I figured the longer we stayed together the better chance I had of being his future wife. It sounds ridiculous, I know, but that's how I thought back them.

As each year passed, one boyfriend after the other, I figured somehow or someway they would see what a great woman I was and would want to marry me. I wanted them to love me and show me what real love looked like, despite how young and unprepared I was. There I was, desperately seeking something from someone, but totally unaware of the true reasons behind my decisions.

Then, in my late twenties, I found myself on the phone going off on somebody during a very heated conversation: "I don't need you anyway! I've never needed you! I'm fine without you! You are a liar! When will you ever apologize for everything you've done to me and for never being there?"

Yeah, that was me yelling on the phone. Back then, it took a lot for me to confront someone, so the fact that I was on the phone yelling and screaming meant I was really fired up. I was so loud that my husband could hear me from the other room. He was confused as to why I was on the phone, so he asked me, "Who is that?"

I mouthed to him, "My dad."

Although I was newly married and happy about starting a new chapter in my life, I was also emotional and sad because my grandmother had just passed away just a few short months after our wedding. Needless to say, I wasn't in the mood for lies and excuses as to why my dad was never around. His attempts to put all the blame on my mother for his absence, who was and has always been there for me, really caused me to lose my temper.

I can't remember exactly what I said to my father during the blow-up, but I remember letting it all out. After going back and forth for awhile, eventually my husband picked up the phone, gave him an earful and hung up on him. All I could do was cry like a little baby, and that's when it hit me...

My dad was the first man to break my heart.

Hence, most of my decisions during most of my single life were motivated by something much deeper than I realized. All I wanted was for someone to undo the hurt he caused me.

It has been quite a few years since that blow-up. I guess you could say we've made our peace with that particular situation and have moved on as best we could, considering that he doesn't always tell the truth or keep his promises. Nonetheless, when I look back on everything from when I lost my virginity to so much more, it helps me to understand so many of my actions when I was single.

I can literally count on one hand, maybe two, the number of times I've seen my father over the course of my life. When I think back to my adolescent and childhood years, I can't recall if and when I saw him. Let's not even begin to discuss child support, because that was something almost unheard of in my experience and something my mother and I couldn't rely on. I remember the few instances when I did see him, because they were so sporadic. It was obvious: the less I saw my father, the less I loved myself.

There was an occasion when the church group took a shopping trip about an hour away from where I lived. I guess he found out through the grapevine, because, lo and behold, I ended up running into him at the store. It was totally random and even more awkward when the other kids who were curious and asked me, "Who is that, Shonda?"

On another occasion, a group of us ran into him at a concert. That time, he was with the youth group from his church. What made that particular incident even more awkward was the fact that he came up to the group and introduced himself as my dad. It shocked everyone, because most of them weren't even aware who he was, let alone that he was my father. Hence, it was no surprise that one of our group leaders responded with great surprise and confusion: "You're Shonda's father?!?"

Of course, I can't forget the time he unexpectedly showed up at our house for prom. My best friend and I were at my mom's house taking pictures with our prom dates and getting ready to head out. Then, we heard a knock and, there he was, standing at the door. I really wasn't in the mood to see or talk to him but that didn't stop him from entering and proceeding to talk to me as though we talked every day and hadn't missed a beat. At this point, I was annoyed and unenthused; but, if you hadn't guessed it by now, the time had come for another awkward moment.

This time my grandparents showed up, so they could get a look at their "grandbaby" before I headed off to the dance. My grandmother, who was very wise, beautiful, and of sound mind, took one look at my dad and asked, "Who is this?" I kid you not. It had been so long since the last time we all had seen him, that my grandmother, who I'm told used to adore my dad when he was dating my mother, didn't even recognize him.

As time went on, I didn't hear from him or see him until a few years after the prom incident and then another few years after that. Yes, that meant he wasn't there during my high school years, he didn't attend my college graduation, and he wasn't invited to my wedding. It wasn't until after the start of my freshman year of college that I remember meeting him at a local Arby's restaurant. That's when he told me he was going to help buy me a new cell phone and a few other things. He had never contributed anything before, and as one would have expected, it never happened.

"Keep in touch. You know I'd love to hear from you. I promise I'll do this or that…" That's what he used to tell me when I saw him. All of the random interactions, awkward conversations, and once-in-awhile meet-ups, only reminded me of all of the broken promises. It was as if I were constantly on an emotional roller coaster. It was a reminder of how much he wasn't there and how little he cared. The only consistent thing about my dad was his inconsistency. Little did I know those emotional roller coasters would later play out in my own dating life.

.

Although I might not have "acted out" or been as promiscuous as other girls, I'm willing to bet most of us shared the same struggle: We didn't feel the love from the first man we thought would give it to us the most. Nonetheless, we spent much of our lives trying to increase our self-love or find love through others.

For years, I tried to act tough and acted as if the absence of my father didn't have an effect on me. I avoided going to that vulnerable place because I didn't want to give him credit for anything, whether good or bad. I didn't want to admit that my father broke my heart or that I struggled emotionally because of it. So, I wore the façade and tried to mask it.

Eventually, I had to be honest with myself and admit that, in fact, his absence did have an effect on me. I had to come to terms with the realization that my father was the first man who broke my heart and that I was doing what I could to find and be with someone who wouldn't break his promises or break my heart like he did.

The only problem was I lacked the guidance from the man who was supposed to show me things, like how a man should treat a woman, how to tell if a man truly loved me, or why I shouldn't take guys too seriously too soon. Even though my mom did a great job of raising me and poured as much good sense into me as much as she could, it didn't negate the fact that I still missed the security of a father's protection and approval. Even though I had my granddaddy around and other father figures to look up to, I missed the main man in my life. All of that helped reveal why I yearned so deeply for a love I never knew. Throughout my single life, I was on a quest to find approval from everyone else and, sometimes, at any cost.

Even at the young age of fourteen, I was that girl who thought sexual activity would provide the approval from guys I so desperately craved. When I gave up my "flower," as some people like to call it, I gave up my innocence. After it was all said and done, I felt regretful but I also felt somewhat accomplished. It was odd. I felt like I was the "apple of his eye" and that losing my virginity made me more like an adult, even though I was far from being one. I put my self-love in the hands of a someone who knew as little about self-love and self-respect as I did. We didn't do it because we were in love or because it felt great. We did it because I wanted validation. I figured the more attention the better—whether that attention was good or not.

As that young girl, and even beyond that, I thought the mere act of casual sex actually meant the presence of love. I did not even realize that so-called "love" wasn't the type I was searching for, anyway. I didn't understand then how risky it was for me to do what I did and the consequences that could have taken place: pregnancy, STDs, emotional confusion. If I could go back and talk to my fourteen-year-old self, I would tell her to get up, go home, and don't give up her flower. I would tell her it's not worth the risk and to wait for someone who would actually take care of that gift and take care of her. I wasn't ready for that.

> *"Note to self:*
> *Usually the way we*
> *allow others to treat*
> *us is a reflection of*
> *how much, or how*
> *little, we love and*
> *value ourselves."*

Throughout my latter teenage years and twenties, I tried filling that void. I searched for love in all the wrong places with all the wrong people. It's funny looking back now. I have to admit, as a young teenager I expected young boys to be men and provide for me what I couldn't get from my dad and to also give to me what I couldn't give to myself: self-love. I can even recall "talking" and going out with a guy who was much older than I, but who was pretty deep into the drug game. I didn't care—well at first I didn't—that at times I was in his car and at any moment the police could have pulled us over. I didn't care that he had a baby mama at home who was much older than I was. I figured that, since he had his own money and car, he could take care of and provide for me what my biological father never did.

All I cared about was reassurance. I wanted to know he thought I was beautiful or that he loved me. As I got older, I used to think that if he knew everything about my past hurt and pain, then he would want to be different from the others and try to make me whole and better. Little did I know I presented myself to others as a potential project instead of a potential mate, which made me even more susceptible to heartache.

Eventually, I learned just how difficult it is to love someone else if you don't first love yourself. Usually the way we allow others to treat us is a reflection of how much, or how little, we love and value ourselves. That's why I used to allow certain guys to treat me the way they did, or I would allow certain things to go on for so long.

On the exterior, I seemed like a young lady who had it all and was strong-willed; but, internally, I was yearning for their love and approval. Sometimes I made it so they could easily see it. I used to think I needed a man to complete me and to make me whole, not realizing my wholeness couldn't be manufactured by a relationship or a certain guy. Instead, all of my being and the woman I was supposed to be was because of who and how God made me.

Although it's nice to have love and companionship, I realized I was beautiful and special whether I was with someone or not; but, it took awhile for me to get there. At times, we're not aware of our self-worth, because of things that happened in our childhood or because of the way certain people treated or neglected us. Other times, we know our worth, but we struggle to show ourselves worthy to other people, and then they end up treating us like we're worthless. We settle for mediocre relationships, even though we deserve meaningful relationships.

There was a time when I allowed others to treat me like a rag doll. I let guys play games and manipulate me or use me when they wanted to. When I thought of myself as a queen, however, I started being treated like a queen.

I remember there was a guy who I used to date…wait, I can't even really use the term date because we never went out. Instead, it was more a situation of my showing up if he called, no matter what I was doing. I didn't ask questions, nor did he. We didn't have deep conversations or anything like that. Even the way he talked to me was disrespectful, but I just figured any attention was better than no attention. My lack of self-respect and self-love didn't require anything more than what he was giving me at the moment.

I let it go on for at least a few months, until I finally realized I wasn't taking care of me or my "flower" yet again—and all because I craved the attention. Now, I realize who we are today influences whom we spend our lives with tomorrow. We attract certain types of people based on our actions and behavior. So, even though he was attracted to me, that wasn't enough for what I truly deserved.

Although my father's absence contributed to my absence of self-esteem, I know it's not enough to blame him or anyone else and to go through life using that as an excuse without looking within myself as well. Self-respect has everything to do with me. A lot of us struggle with self-love for one reason or another: daddy wasn't there; mom wasn't there; parents never built you up or encouraged you; you used to be with an abusive man; you were bullied throughout your formative years… The list goes on and on. Whatever it is, we have to own up to it, deal with it, and move on as best as we can.

I don't look back on these experiences merely to talk bad about my father or to make him look bad. I don't want to play the victim for the rest of my life. When I look back on these stories, it's merely to reflect, to learn from them, to move on, and, I hope, to help someone else. Just like with an addict, the first step is admitting there is a problem. So, I had to do just that—admit there was a problem within myself. Yes, my father wasn't there and, yes, he made mistakes. So, I had to ask myself "Why?" But more importantly, I had to ask, "Now, what?" What was I going to do to try and fix my issues?

Sometimes we end up breaking the curse and changing our habits; but, sometimes we do the complete opposite and end up repeating the same mistakes from our past situations. Worst case, we end up becoming or running into the very thing we tried so hard to run away from. That's part of the reason why I dated the types of guys I dated. Unbeknownst to me at the time, some of those guys emulated some of the same behavior and characteristics of my dad, even though they were some of the same traits I tried so hard to avoid.

Eventually, I vowed that I wouldn't marry a man who reminded me of my father. I wanted to break the curse and make sure my future children didn't grow up without a father. In doing that, however, I still had to take responsibility for my own actions especially those times when I chose to listen to my peers instead of my mom or when I did things merely to get attention. At some point in my life, I realized my self-esteem had everything to do

17

with me and what I thought of myself, despite what others said or did to me. It wasn't enough for me go from guy to guy, thinking they would provide everything I needed. I learned to stop allowing my father's absence to dictate my present situation and how I felt about myself.

The same is true even now when it comes to my relationship with my husband. I can't project my past feelings onto my present situation with him. As a married woman, I have to remind myself that my husband isn't a replacement for my father; conversely, I can't allow my fears and hesitations to keep us from moving forward within our marriage.

For example, I remember shortly after we got married and started talking more about our future and family. I was so adamant about not having children so quickly. At first my husband, Eric, didn't understand my reluctance and, quite honestly, I didn't understand it either. Why was I so against having children? Yes, the fact that I wanted to do more and enjoy being married first was a part of it, but the reason went deeper than that once we discussed it further.

When you're raised by a single mom, sometimes things get hard. Everyday you see your mom (or dad, for the single dads out there) working so hard to provide for her family and doing the best she can. Meanwhile, your dad is off living his life and doing what he wants. Eric, on the other hand was raised by both his mother and father who are still married to this day. So, while he thought of children as a blessing, I thought of them more as a burden. He was concerned with having a family, but I was more concerned with how much goes into raising a child. Quite honestly, I was scared and thought Eric would be like my father and leave me to raise the children all by myself. It may sound harsh, but that's how much my father's absence affected me. Truth be told, a lot of others could say the same.

I know in the Bible it speaks about children being a gift from God, but much of what I associated with children was struggle— in my own life and the lives of most of my closest and dearest friends who also came from single-parent homes. Nevertheless, my husband had to remind me that he was not my father. He was serious about the vows we made before God, and he was serious about raising a family with me, not without me.

I also have to remember my husband isn't a replacement for my father. As much as he loves and cares for me, at the end of the day, he is not one hundred percent responsible for my self-esteem, nor is he responsible for the mistakes my father made.

Thankfully, about a year or so before I met my husband, I figured out how to love myself—by myself. Because he is the main man in my life, it's important, of course, that he encourages me and makes me feel good about myself. So, on days when I don't feel my prettiest or when I'm down on myself, it's nice to hear him say, "You're the most beautiful woman." However, I still understand that my self-esteem has everything to do with what I think of myself–inside and out–and not just what he thinks.

Finding self-love is all about finding those qualities, characteristics, and features–inside and out–within ourselves that make us unique and beautiful. It's less about what society says we should look like and more about God's love reflected through us. Self-love focuses more on what we love about ourselves and less on what others may think. It's less about comparing myself to other people, and more about others being able to see my true beauty and being with someone who will love me for me.

For me, personally, it is about embracing the kind-hearted, giving, loving, and genuine person I am. I embrace my thick curves, my long, natural hair, and my brown skin (even though people often like to remind me of how light or high yellow I am). I embrace my spiritual gifts as well as my natural born talents. I embrace all of it.

I say all of that, not with arrogance or to boast, but to thank God, because I am finally able to see the beauty that lies within and the qualities and personality He specifically designed for me. Do I have days when I don't feel as beautiful–whether inside or out? Absolutely. However, it's not something that makes me feel broken; and, it's definitely not something that will cause me to allow someone else to bring me down.

20

When it comes to having more self-esteem, there are five things we can do to work on it:

1. Admit who or what hurt you in the past or contributed to your low self-esteem (confront your issues).
2. Ask God and/or seek professional assistance to help heal your heart from past pain.
3. Accentuate and remind yourself of your best qualities, features, and accomplishments.
4. Avoid people who are committed to tearing you down.
5. Accept and love yourself by accepting nothing but the best.

Find out what you love about yourself. What makes you stand out? What makes you different? Don't wait for someone to tell you something you should already know about yourself. You are more than a sidepiece. You are more than "booty call" or a one-night stand. You are more than your hair, your physical features, or your Instagram naked pictures. You are more and you deserve more.

We cannot expect to be happy with someone else if we can't first be happy with ourselves. Moreover, if we find it hard to be happy for someone else, then it's likely because we're not happy with ourselves.

As a married woman, there is no happy "we" without a happy "me" (and vice versa). I realized a long time ago that my unhealthy search for love was because of my unhealthy self-love.

No longer can we rely on others to do or provide what we can't even do or provide for ourselves. Don't become so dependent on someone else that you forget how to love yourself.

Lesson Two

Let it flow, but don't get stuck in the gray area.

It's was roughly eight o'clock and we had just sat down for dinner. This was a first date, which can be pretty intimidating and awkward, but this time I was looking forward to it.

I was rocking my cute little jeans, top, and stilettos. He wore a nice, button-down shirt, jeans, and some nice looking casual sneakers. We covered basic small talk and discussed our school majors, our interests, our extra-curricular activities, our hometowns, our families, and so on. Then, he asked, "So, when is the last time you've been in a relationship?"

I responded with, "Well, the last one I was in wasn't that great. I found out he was cheating and lying to me. He really broke my heart." I continued on about what I wanted in a relationship, my past hurts, my ex-boyfriends, and so on. I told him what I wanted in a future husband and when I wanted to get married and all that good stuff. I probably went on for what seemed like hours, but he was polite and continued listening to each one of my grunts, complaints, and wishes.

The date continued and we talked for a long time. We discussed his past relationships and what he was looking for in a girlfriend and how he wanted to get to know me and vice versa. We laughed, we talked, ate dinner, and he even asked to see me again. We ended the date with a nice hug and parted ways.

I headed to my car and, before I could even make it back to my apartment, I called up my girlfriend and gave her all the juicy details. That was pretty typical for every date.

"Oh my goodness, I think I found the one!" I told her excitedly.

"The one?!" she exclaimed, "I mean…I guess. Just take your time." She was being polite.

"I know, I know, but he was so nice and polite and he said he wants to go out again." I told her. "I've never had that much fun on a date before. I think this is it, girl!"

A few weeks passed. We saw each other on the weekends and talked every few days or so. Things seemed to be going pretty well, but I was getting anxious, as usual. I was ready to move forward, even though it had only been a few, short weeks.

One night we were on the phone talking and I thought there was no better time than then to ask him the dreaded question. So, I did.

"So, what are we doing? Are we boyfriend and girlfriend or what?"

He responded, "Uh, what do you mean, what are we?" I could hear the confusion in his voice. "I thought everything was cool and we were enjoying each other's company for now."

"Well, don't think I'm just going to be sitting around waiting on you forever. I know it's only been a few weeks, but I don't want to be single forever."

I was getting angry and he was becoming more and more confused.

The conversation continued for a while. We went back and forth and debated about what we were doing, what was our status, when were we going to be exclusive, and all that good stuff. Eventually, it turned into an argument.

Needless to say, that was the last time I heard from him.

> "Note to self: Quit trying to rush it. Learn how to let it flow."

It's probably safe to say I never heard from that guy again because I probably scared him off. After all of the talking and sharing I did during the first date, I'm surprised I even got a second date. Now, there I was only a few weeks in and already questioning the status of the relationship and trying to force him to make a decision. Not that it can't happen, but I wasn't even sure he was someone I truly wanted to be with after that short amount of time.

I used to think I could foreshadow how the relationship would go based on the first date, until I realized and heard a great quote: "Every potential date is not a potential mate." Call me crazy, but I honestly used to think if the date went well, then maybe it was a sign he was my future husband. I used to obsess about the status of the relationship.

Because I desperately wanted to be in a relationship (and now we know why), I wanted to take things to the next level as soon as possible. I later discovered through my single season that sometimes we psych ourselves out of a good thing by trying to force something to happen. I have experienced situations and have known people who were so obsessed with what was going to happen, that they totally missed what was happening.

Furthermore, it's a turn off to most men. Men don't want to feel like they're being coerced or rushed into something. That's why I believe the Bible says, "He who finds a wife finds a good thing" (Proverbs 18:22). The woman isn't trying to push him down the aisle or make him be with her. If she does, he will most likely end up regretting it or harbor resentment towards her. That's not to say that we should wait on someone forever; but if it feels right and it's flowing right, then play it cool and let it happen. Let the conversations and natural progression of the relationship flow.

Although my question of "what are we doing" may have been a valid question for later on down the road, the timing wasn't necessarily the best. As a woman, I've learned that some men don't necessarily think about getting married or being in a long-term relationship like we do or as much as we do. As little girls, we were conditioned to constantly think about the type of man we wanted to marry, our wedding, our dream house, etc., while little boys were more concerned with GI Joe and Transformers. By the time I met my husband, I learned even more how to just let it flow and what that looked like for me.

When we met, I decided I was not going to obsess over our relationship status. No lie: I made a vow to myself. We talked on the phone and dated, but I was cool and calm about everything. It was like I was sailing on water even though I don't like to go on cruise ships. About a month or so later, to my surprise, he asked me to be exclusive. Then, and only then, did I have to really consider the status of our relationship. Most times before that, I was usually the one trying to take things to the next level, but this time was different.

Even then, I was still hesitant because I didn't want to rush into anything; but, boy, was it refreshing to have him take the initiative this time around. I didn't have to worry about where we stood, if I was his girl, or if he wanted to be with me. Besides the fact that he was going away for awhile and he wanted me all to himself being that I was a new girl in a

> "Note to self: Never assume what has yet to be acknowledged."

27

new city, I honestly think my resistance to rush it played a role in his decision to want to take things to the next level.

Although I had to learn how to let it flow, I also learned how to determine when it was time to stop letting it flow. In other words, I used to have a habit of acting as if things were something they weren't… and I'm not talking about having faith and speaking certain things into existence.

There were times when I found myself in countless situations where I was caught up and confused. I often found myself in a place that I like to call the "gray area." Think about the colors - white, black, and gray (a mixture of both).

When you are in the white stage, it is like a blank canvas. It's just two people starting out and getting to know each other. Then, there's the black canvas. This signifies that the white canvas has been filled in. In other words, both parties are exclusively and unequivocally committed to each other.

Then, you have the gray area and that's where things can get really confusing and it can have different meanings for different people. The gray area can mean two people are dating, but not exclusive. It could mean two people just met and they are, for a lack of better words, just messing around or just talking. Another example could mean both parties are growing closer but one of them may be hesitant to take the relationship to the next level. Those who who fear commitment or going to the next level often use the gray area for this purpose because it is the perfect place to camp out for awhile without any obligation.

While the gray area can work for a certain period of time and for some people, it becomes difficult when things are left open for miscommunication or misinterpretation. For instance, sometimes we assume we're in a relationship, while the other person thinks we're just friends. Even though we're doing things as if we are in a relationship, we fail to acknowledge the true status of the relationship. Oftentimes, we end up in the gray area because we allow ourselves to get into or stay in situations without setting any clear expectations.

I remember when I dated a guy for about eight months without ever truly knowing what our status was. It was obvious we were in the gray stage but I was confused as to what was really going on. I thought I was his girlfriend and we were exclusive because we did almost everything together. We went on dates during the week. We studied together, we cooked together, attended parties and dances together and we even took mini trips together. I figured since we were doing things in the public eye and he was treating me like his girl, then I must have been his girl, but little did I know that was not the case. I assumed something that had yet been acknowledged.

Interestingly enough, later I found out he was involved with a number of females but finally decided to be exclusive with one of them that I was not aware of. Imagine my confusion and frustration when I received a phone call telling me he was in an exclusive relationship with someone else. How could he be in an exclusive relationship with someone else when all the while I thought we were? I was devastated and so hurt.

That taught me a lesson though - men will do what you allow them to do. I failed to discuss his and my expectations in the beginning, which meant I entered into a relationship without really knowing exactly what he eventually wanted from the relationship or what, if anything, we were working toward in the future. I failed to clearly communicate and discuss my expectations, because I feared that if I had, then I would've been rejected.

It was during that time when I had to decide for myself how long was too long to wait and how soon was too soon to discuss expectations. Obviously a few weeks was a bit too soon for me, but eight months was entirely too long to go on thinking I was with someone who was not with me. Metaphorically speaking, I basically wasted a lot of time driving around in circles trying to get to a destination when I could've just stopped and asked for directions sooner to make sure we were both headed in the same direction.

While it's important to let things flow, it's also important to have some type of idea of where things are headed. Don't end up like I did in either situation, trying to force things to happen so fast that you end up chasing people away or entering into something without having a clear understanding of expectations.

Even if you are looking for a relationship, it does not have to begin immediately. Take time to get to know him and yourself, before you assume he wants the same things. Had I taken more time in the beginning and been wiser with my decisions, ultimately, it could have saved me some time and humiliation in the end. When all is said and done, sometimes you have to let it flow and sometimes you have to let it go.

Lesson Three

Don't think of him as a piece of clay that you can mold into what you want him to be.

"Hey, John, what's up?"

"Nothing, girl. What's up with you, sexy? I was wondering if you were going to call me."

"Yeah, I know. But I thought you were talking to somebody else. I didn't know you liked me like that."

"Nah, I'm single. What's up with you, though? We trying to do this or what?"

"Do what?"

"You know what. I'm trying to see you and your fine self."

"I don't know, John. I mean, I guess I can, but not if you're with somebody."

"How many times I have to tell you? I ain't with nobody. I'm trying to get with you. Quit playing, girl. We already talked about this the other day."

"I mean, I guess. So, when you want me to come over?"

"What about tomorrow? And wear those cute jeans you wore the other day."

"Okay, I'll be there tomorrow."

"Cool. I hope you're ready for me."

"Whatever. You're crazy. I'll talk to you later."

"Cool. See you later." The call ends.

Samantha clicks over. "Shonda, did you hear all that?"

"Yeah, I heard it." I admitted, embarrassed.

Little did "John" know, I had just witnessed a 3-way phone call with my so-called boyfriend trying to hook up with another girl.

"Note to self: I can only change the things I have the power to change."

Prior to that phone call, "Samantha" recently heard "John" and I were together, even though he had pursued her at the same time. She was unaware about us until she heard about it through the grapevine. So, she decided to warn me.

So, we did what any mature young ladies would do. We did it the old school way: setup a 3-way call and catch him red-handed. (This was before texting and screenshots were available.) Of course, I was angry, hurt, and confused. I wanted so much to be mad at her, but I really didn't have a reason to be. I respected the fact that she came to me and told me the truth.

Here I was thinking I had a boyfriend, only to realize not even a week later that he was trying to date another girl. I could not believe it. Never once did he mention my name or anything about us during their conversation.

You know what's even crazier than that? I ended up staying with this guy for at least a few years after this call. It wasn't like we were married and needed to at least try and work through it. I could've easily started over and moved on with someone else, but instead I chose to stay with him. Why? Because I thought I could change him. I thought I could do anything and everything to make him want to be with me.

It has been one of the hardest lessons, but I know now more than ever that you can't change a person or make him do something he don't want to do. You definitely can't make him be with someone with whom he doesn't want to be.

It is awe-inspiring to sit and watch an actual potter mold his dull and messy clay into a beautiful piece of art. What starts off looking a muddy mess later turns into a wonderful pot, cup, plate, or whatever the potter chooses to create. Once the work is complete, we place the finished product in our homes or on our shelves as an exhibit for others to see.

The potter of course did not create the clay, but he put great effort into creating a piece of work that will please him and others will enjoy. We must realize, however, the potter is working with clay and not humans, so it is unrealistic to think we, as humans, can do the same with other people.

When I taught high school for a short-lived year, I remember how difficult it was to change the students' way of thinking, especially since they were in high school. I would try and show them the opportunities available and encourage them to envision a better future, despite their backgrounds. But it wasn't easy to convince them. They had already developed a certain mindset based on their environment, their peers, and their upbringing.

Although I succeeded with some and I knew I had the power to influence their thoughts and behavior, ultimately, I knew they had to decide to change on their own. I couldn't force them to do it. It's quite possible, had I stayed longer, that maybe I would've had more of an impact on them. Regardless, it was up to them to decide for themselves. The same is true in relationships.

Change is a good thing when a person realizes the need for it and decides to modify his or her lifestyle or actions. However, conflict ensues when we try to force people to do what they don't want to do. While we can influence change and inspire others to change, one thing we cannot do is to force them to change.

Take my story at the beginning of the chapter. Following the incident with the 3-way call and the secret hook-up (I'm not sure if they ever did or not), there were more incidents after that. The rumors and lies continued throughout the duration of our relationship, but I stayed. I was convinced I could change his way of thinking. I thought he would get tired of the other girls and decide to be with me only. Of course he wasn't completely innocent. He would lie and tell me he was going to change, but his actions never matched his words. Sometimes he would do okay for a little bit, and then he was back at it again. This was the pattern for a long time.

I made myself believe that all the other girls—and there were plenty—he messed with were minor compared to me. I made excuses for his behavior and contented myself with the fact that, at the end of the day, he came back to me. However, I had to be honest with myself about the fact that he was coming back to me *after* he had been with at least two or three other females. Although it was clear he wasn't ready to be with one woman, I ignored the signs.

I used to justify my position as his number one girl out of the group, but who really wants to share her man with another woman? I didn't. If I've learned anything about love, it's that you don't have to worry about being number one when you know you are the only one.

I didn't understand it at the time, but I was worth more than just a name added to his list of girls. Had I realized a long time ago that I couldn't change a man or make one be with me, I would've saved myself a lot of heartache, disappointment, and time.

If you're anything like me, you may know the types of thoughts that went through my mind, or the things I thought about doing to try to force a man to be with me or to try to change him. Just to name a few, what about:

- ❖ If I give up the goods, he'll want to be with me.
- ❖ If I get his name tattooed on my body, he'll be with me.
- ❖ If I take him back one more time, he'll be with me.
- ❖ If he gets with me, then he'll change.
- ❖ If I do everything he asks, no matter the cost, he'll be with me.
- ❖ If I repeatedly yell at him about going to church, then he'll go with me.
- ❖ If I force him to go ring shopping, then he'll marry me.
- ❖ If I force him to marry me, then he'll stay with me.
- ❖ If I have his baby, then he'll really marry me.

There's a difference between influencing change and forcing change. Believe me, I'm a living witness that people can in fact transform their lives over time. However, I also understand we can only change those things we have the power to change. If someone is a certain way when you meet him, then he or she will likely remain that way throughout the relationship.

38

Even when it comes to marriage, if your spouse was like that before you got married, then don't expect for it to change just because you decided to get married. When we meet the one or are considering it, that's when we have to decide what we can live with and what we may have to part with.

Instead of thinking my ex was going to change,

> **"Note to self: There's a difference between influencing change and forcing change."**

despite all of the lies and cheating, I could have easily changed my role and removed myself from the situation altogether. Instead of trying to change his mindset, I should've changed my mindset.

There are times, I must admit, when we can influence change without having to pressure the other person. When Eric and I started dating, he knew how important my spirituality and my personal relationship with God was. I'll never forget when he told me, "I'm a man of God first, before anything." You know how they say, "He had me at hello?" Well, he had me at, "I'm a man of God."

I was elated to hear this. He was honest with me and admitted that he knew God and had a personal relationship with Him, but he hadn't been going to church, reading his Bible, or praying like he used to. He didn't feel as spiritually connected as I did. For some, the red light would've flared—and it did for a split second—but it didn't cause a conflict between us. Instead, it was something we both worked through.

Although I don't believe going to church makes anyone any more saved than the next person, I do believe in fellowship, serving and ministry, learning, teaching, growing, and witnessing. Plus, I know all too well how much of an impact the church and my relationship with God has had on my own spiritual journey. That, among a number of other things, is why I'm still here today.

Nevertheless, I didn't harass him or try to force him to do anything. I believe all of us have different journeys and we all grow at different levels. Just because I had been in church all my life didn't make me any better than he. He didn't need my judgment, and who was I to judge anyway, considering my past?

The best thing I could do was show him the love of Christ through my words and through my actions. Sometimes the best way for us to witness to others is not so much in what we say, but what we do. Besides, I knew if it had been me, I wouldn't have wanted someone constantly berating me about my spiritual life or going to church. So, I just prayed for him and we openly talked about it in a way that was comfortable for him.

Then, one day I received a phone call while he was in Ohio for graduate school. He called to tell me he found a church and decided to join under watch care (For those of you who may not be familiar, watch care is a temporary dedication to a local church). I was so excited and so proud of him! God was moving in his life. During one of my visits, I was able to go and attend church with him.

About a year or so later, Eric was back in Atlanta and, as if things couldn't get any better, he decided to re-dedicate his life to Christ! He wanted to get baptized. I know…cue the tears. I still remember when we went shopping for some all-white pants for the big day. His parents and some of our dear friends joined us for that special night.

Everything happened according to God's plan. Some people would have assumed something like that would've pushed us away from each other in the beginning; but, instead, it made us even that much closer. None of this happened because I forced him to do it. Rather it happened because he wanted to do it. Besides, the more we try to impose certain things on other people, the more it can lead to resentment and bitterness.

Just like I didn't force Eric to be with me, I should've realized sooner that I couldn't force other guys to be with me. It took me some time, but later it was clear that you have to begin as you mean to go on, as the old saying goes. My decision to stay with certain people, despite all of the mess, only encouraged the behavior.

> **"Note to self: If a man wants to be with you, he'll be with you."**

Eventually, I empowered myself and learned that, if I couldn't control his actions and behavior, then I would change what I had the power to control–me. I stopped lowering my standards and expectations just to cater to people who were unwilling to change.

There's a well-known prayer called "The Serenity Prayer." It simply says: "Lord, please grant me the serenity to accept those things I cannot change, the courage to change the things I can, and the wisdom to know the difference." It doesn't get any more real than that. If we can sincerely pray this prayer and acknowledge that we have no power to truly change someone, then we can accept God's plans for our lives instead of trying to force things that weren't meant to be in the first place.

One of the greatest lessons I've learned about love is this simple truth: if a man wants to be with you, he'll be with you. He won't make excuses. He won't play games. He won't try to manipulate you. Men will make it very clear to you if they want to be with you. He will do what it takes to get you and keep you because: A) he will want to and B) because he won't be able to stand the thought of seeing you with someone else.

If someone keeps saying he's going to do things differently, but you don't see the modifications, then that could mean it's time for you to make a change instead of wasting your energy trying to change that person.

Sometimes, when people say "no" to you, they're saying "no" to themselves because they're not ready to step up to the next level in the relationship or even within their own lives. That's okay, because life goes on.

Lesson Four

Don't expect different results
using the same habits.

One day during my college years, I walked in and found a letter from two of my dear friends. It read something like this:

"Hey, Shonda. We're writing this letter, first and foremost, to let you know we love you and we care about you and we don't want to see you hurt. However, it has come to our attention that your boyfriend is cheating with another girl, and she is pregnant."

The letter went on to describe who their sources were and how they were one hundred percent sure of the truth. At first, I didn't want to believe it, and, of course, my boyfriend wouldn't own up to anything. I figured they were just jealous and they didn't want to see me happy.

A few days later, he finally admitted it was true. I guess he figured he had to, since the soon-to-be mother of his child and I ended up in the same class together later that summer. Needless to say, I broke up with him and, of course, I apologized to my friends.

Fast forward to a few years later…different guy, different time of my life.

I had a late night "pack your stuff and let's ride out" type of night. You know those times, ladies, when you do a creep drive-by or pop up unannounced to catch them off guard. Okay, not you? Well, I *was* that lady at one time in my life.

It was around 12:00 a.m. and I was lying in bed. The same dear friends who warned me about the other "baby mama drama" incident had stopped by to share with me another incident about my latest boyfriend. I don't know how the information always seemed to find its way to them, but it was inevitable that God made it so that such bad news came from them versus strangers, which, in the end, meant that it came from a reliable source. As if the last situation wasn't enough for me, what they told me was the last thing I wanted to hear. But I listened anyway. I learned the hard way the last time.

They described to me an instance when he had tried to come on to another young lady whom we knew very well and told me about these secret parties that had been taking place. That time, I was ready to confront him and I had my witnesses with me.

It was late, but it just so happened I knew exactly where he was. So, I did what came naturally. I threw on some clothes, we hopped into the car, and I drove to his apartment totally unannounced. This time, I was going to confront the issue head-on. (I wouldn't necessarily suggest the same for someone else, but, hey, I had a moment.)

Upon reaching his place, I confronted him. The discussion devolved into a yelling match in which I did most of the yelling.

What was funny about all of this was that it hadn't been the first time I had to deal with something like that with him. Obviously, it wasn't my proudest moment and it was quite embarrassing when I think back on it. After all of the yelling and screaming and after I shed my tears and cried myself to sleep that night, I finally told myself, "Never again!"

> **"Note to self: Good men aren't bad habits."**

I cannot deny the fault of these men and how horrible they treated me, despite how loyal and faithful I was to them. However, I can honestly say I often found myself in those types of situations because of their bad habits as well as my own. I often allowed things to go on for longer than they should have, and I almost always gave guys too many chances.

Even with the two stories I mentioned in this chapter, I already knew what was going on. I had an inkling (or what was likely feminine intuition) that something wasn't right; but, instead of confronting the issues, I stayed doing the same old thing with the same people. I found myself repeating the pattern over and over, dating the same type of guy or doing the same type of things. At the end of the day, no matter how many relationships I had been in, I was the common denominator. It was a hard truth to swallow, but it was the truth nonetheless.

At one point, every relationship started off practically the same and looked just like the previous one. I started to believe that constant drama, constant heartache, and constant confusion were normal for a relationship. I figured that even if I did the same things with a different guy, the next guy would appreciate it more than the last. I really didn't change whom I dated or how I dated. I definitely didn't change how I allowed them to treat me.

It's interesting, because sometimes when you're used to being treated a certain way or you're used to a certain way of life, you start to think that's how it's supposed to be. Even worse, you begin to believe that's what you deserve. Just because we may be used to one way doesn't mean we don't deserve a better way. Good men aren't bad habits. Good men don't create situations in which we're constantly going back and forth or questioning our decision to stay or move on.

Case in point: how many times have we had to constantly check a man's phone, check his email or social media, sneak and drive to his house to see if he was home or to see if some other girl was over there?

Whether we're willing to admit it or not, some of us, unfortunately, have had our Jazmine Sullivan moments: "I bust the windows out your car." Personally, I've never broken a car window, keyed a car, or put sand in the gas tank, but there have definitely been occasions when my exes or certain relationships took me to a place where I was ready to do whatever needed to be done.

As I got older, I realized having a good man means having good habits–both on his side and my side. In other words, I don't have to question his every move or constantly check his email, phone calls, text messages, or social media. Now, as husband and wife, do we check in on each other every now and then to make sure we are good? Absolutely. Do I have his passwords and codes (and vice versa)? Absolutely. But we trust each other and suspicion is not something that constantly consumes our minds, thoughts, or behaviors.

Moreover, we're not driving each other to the point of no return. I'm not chasing him around the city to see where he is and we're not constantly arguing about some random sidepiece that's trying to get with my man. We're not creating bad habits for each other.

When I told myself, "never again," I promised myself I would never allow a man to treat me like that again. Never again would I keep doing the same things over and over. Never again would I keep dating the same type of guys. It was time to break my habits and do something different. I even wrote a poem to myself to remind me to never go down that road again.

Never again.

You broke my heart, but not my spirit.

I let you take my happiness for awhile, but not anymore because I'm too pretty not to smile.

I feel so lonely and confused, but thank God I'm never alone.

You hurt me so bad, but this, too, shall pass.

You made me cry, but God will wipe the tears from my eyes.

I sacrificed so much for you, but God will replenish.

Everything you took from me, God will restore back to me.

You diminished my trust in men, but thank God I still trust in the man above.

You controlled me with lies and manipulation, but God still controls my destination.

Right now it's hard for me to see anything but me and you, but I still believe there will be a breakthrough.

Not anymore.

Never again.

No more waiting.

Never again.

I was over it and had had enough. I was done with making myself think he was going to stop lying and cheating or that he was going to change his bad habits. I stopped trying to convince myself it was meant to be when I knew it wasn't. I was done with meeting up with guys or inviting them over to my place just because I wanted someone there.

When I started dating Eric, I really decided to do things differently. I refused to accept anything less than what I deserved. I could not practice the same habits from before. I had to change them. Basically, I made him work for my love–something I had never really done before. No longer did I accept the bare minimum or allow guys to treat me any kind of way. Not only was I concerned about the habits of the person whom I was with, but I was even more concerned about my own personal habits.

You know another bad habit I had? I used to mistake projects for prospects. I called things relationships, even though they were really just "situation-ships."

With any project, whether work-related or personal, oftentimes we try to find a resolution or fix something that's wrong, only to later realize that it can't be fixed. I often found myself in these types of situations. I thought I was Iyanla Vanzant and tried to fix people's lives. I figured I could straighten certain people out or get them on the right path, even if they felt neither concern nor need to better themselves. They were fine just the way they were.

"Situation-ships" were those instances in which I treated men like relationships but they were merely relationship fillers. They occupied space in my life, but they weren't meaningful, and they were going nowhere fast. I spent a lot of time trying to improve people who I knew weren't meant to be in my life forever.

I was the woman that would hang onto something forever, despite how confusing and never-ending it seemed. There was no end in sight. Aaliyah Dana Haughton said in one of her songs, "We need a resolution." But there wasn't one.

If you're anything like me or how I used to be, then you, too, may be feeling stuck or feel like you just keep going around and around in circles with a certain someone. If so, it's very likely you're stuck in a situation-ship. Situation-ships make us feel good for the moment; but then the feeling passes away as soon as they leave or as soon as we take just enough time to consider and ask ourselves, "What am I really doing with him? Why am I still going through this?"

They're tricky because they have a way of making us feel like it's normal and a part of our everyday lives. They make us feel as if we're in a committed relationship, when it's the complete opposite. They trick us into thinking the wait is worth it, even though we have no idea if or when they will ever commit. It forces us to put up with things for so long that, eventually, we forget what it even feels like to be in a real relationship. Don't let the situation-ships fool you. You're either in a relationship or you're not.

We have to be truthful with ourselves and ask the tough questions in order to start the process of changing the habits. I started asking myself: "What can I do differently? Am I doing too much too soon? What am I allowing to happen that I shouldn't? What is my attitude?" That's when I made a decision to break the habits of staying, waiting, and playing. When we're real with ourselves and start to break old habits, we open ourselves up to new and improved habits.

As if I didn't have enough bad habits of my own, so often I made the mistake of auditioning certain people to play the role as my boyfriend or future husband, knowing good and well they weren't even ready (nor was I) or willing to audition for the role. Plain and simple: you can't audition a boy for the role of a man.

There were situations when I knew the guy was immature, I knew he wasn't ready for a relationship, or I knew we weren't on the same page. Still, I made excuses. It took some time, but I finally realized their manhood was not my responsibility. I could not force anyone to grow up or change. I was responsible for my own actions and what I allowed from others.

> "Note to self:
> You can't audition
> a boy for the role
> of a man."

Even though I went through what seemed like a number of auditions, I can honestly say my husband earned the coveted role. No longer did I have to worry about trying to change boys into men, because he was at a point in his life when he knew what he wanted—and so did I. This time we were on the same page, reading the same book.

There's something wonderful about experiencing the love of a real man at the right time. There's a reason why I say real men aren't afraid of real love. A man who is ready for love will sacrifice himself to take care of you. A man who is ready for love won't have a problem making it known to you and those around him. A man who is ready for love will treat you like a rare diamond, because he understands and values your worth. Someone who values your worth is worth your time.

As a married woman, people often ask me, "How did you know he was 'the one?'" or "How will I know if he's 'the one?'" Whether it's love at first sight, a sign, or a friendship that develops into something greater, everyone has his or her own theory about how to know if the person is truly "the one."

Quite frankly, I personally don't believe there's a "silver bullet" when it comes to true love or when it comes to finding the right guy or vice versa. It's different for everyone and each of us have his or her own story.

Furthermore, discerning between a temporary guy and the man with whom you're destined to spend the rest of your life isn't about finding the perfect person, because that's impossible; rather it's about being with the right person at the right time. I'm not perfect, my husband isn't perfect and our relationship isn't perfect, but we're perfect for each other.

One thing's for certain: when it comes to the real thing, it definitely feels different from anything you've experienced before. For me, it was less about how did I know and more about what was different. Although it's not inclusive of everything, I've listed a few things to provide a glimpse of how I knew my relationship with my husband was different, based on my personal experiences as well as the experiences of some of my other married friends.

8 Signs He Could Be "The One"

His actions will speak louder than his words. There were times when I was left heartbroken and confused because my ex's words didn't align with his actions. Nevertheless, I continued to give it my all and allowed certain things to happen (lies, cheating, etc.), even though the signs were clear and it was obvious he didn't want to be with me. Don't ignore the signs. Green means go. Yellow means caution. Red means stop.

You won't have to beg or force him to be with you. I used to try to force so many things. Ironically, however, when we first started dating, Eric pursued me persistently before I officially became his girlfriend. I wasn't trying to be exclusive with him until he worked out his lingering "situations," especially since I knew he was going to be living in a different city while attending school. Sure enough, he did what he needed to do to convince me. I didn't have to beg him to be with me. I like what Trent Shelton said: "You never have to chase what wants to stay."

Your bad habits will be replaced with good habits, and old emotions replaced with new ones. Sometimes when you're so used to things being a certain way—constantly arguing, never-ending drama—you think that's how it's supposed to be. But when it's the real thing, you quickly realize what you've been missing all along. What used to always feel like constant drama started to feel more like a dream. My tears were replaced with tenderness. My anger and bitterness were replaced with happiness. My worry was replaced with trust. I didn't have to worry about what he was doing and where he was going. A good relationship should bring out the best in you, not the worst.

You will be able to look back at your past relationships as a stepping stone for your new one. Better yet, you may not have to look back at all; only to reflect and thank God for helping you to find the good in the goodbye. I realized my past was merely rehearsal for the present. My husband loves the "hell" out of me in that he loves so much that it seems as if all of the mess I experienced in the past was pushed out and replaced with his love.

You won't have to have to worry about competing for the number one spot because you will be the only one. Eric wasn't afraid to make it known to others—including those whom he used to date—that I was his woman and he was my man. When it was time, we were clear on what we both wanted in the relationship.

You will experience or remember what it feels like to be loved. There's something about real love that makes you remember, or experience for the very first time, what it feels like to love and be loved. Call me "old school," but when we dated, that was practically the first time in my life I knew what it felt like to be treated like a lady by a gentleman. For a long time, I forgot what courting and romance looked like. I forgot how nice it was to receive a hand-written poem versus just a text, but Eric reminded me very quickly.

Even still today, he opens my doors for me, pulls out my chair, and treats me like I've never been treated before. It's easy to think you might've really liked someone, but it's euphoric to know you love someone and he loves you back.

You won't have to be someone you're not, because he'll accept you for who you are. I can be quite a character at times, especially since I'm more of the free spirited, creative type and my husband has more of the "Type A" personality. The good thing is that we balance each other and he doesn't try to force me to be anything else other than my crazy, emotional, driven, extroverted, "trying to do too much" self. He loves me for who I am—flaws and all.

You won't have to question it. It's kind of like the process of searching for a home or even a wedding dress. They always say, "When it's the one, you'll just know." God blessed us with feminine intuition. We know when something doesn't feel right or when something feels good. For me, it's unlike anything else I've ever experienced in my life. Even during the highs and lows of our relationship, it still feels like a breath of fresh air.

Whether we're relaxing at home and acting silly, when we're just talking, when he's wiping my tears because I'm emotional, or when he's taking care of me because I'm sick, I can feel the love. As the dear and wise Maya Angelou once said, "One thing love is not is unsure."

.

Different habits lead to different results. Judge your relationship less on what you're told and more on what you see. When it comes to the real thing, you should be able to see a difference in your relationship.

Lesson Five

Don't confuse love with lust.

Our eyes met on the dance floor and immediately you could feel the chemistry and the connection. After a late night of dancing and club-hopping, we met back at my apartment and talked. We talked and talked and talked some more until the sun rose. He told me about his past experiences as well as his future dreams and his goals and aspirations, as did I.

We connected and related to each other on so many levels. It felt different—unlike anything I ever experienced before. It was truly one of the best nights of my life!

Shortly thereafter, we started dating. The attraction was evident and so intense. He was so fine it made him practically irresistible. Then, one night he came over to my apartment and we were in my bedroom kissing heavily and caressing each other. One thing led to the next and then it happened.

I was much older by then (mid to late twenties) and even though I knew what I was doing this time around, I still questioned myself, almost like the first time. There I was again, laying with a man I didn't really know that well and doing something I had struggled with my entire life since the age of fourteen. All of us have our own struggles; this was the one I struggled with most.

I was torn and conflicted about what I was doing, so much so that I started crying. I'm sure it totally freaked him out. Immediately he asked, "Why are you crying? Did I do something wrong?" He hadn't done anything wrong, but I felt like I was doing everything wrong. I was about to do the same thing I had done in all of my other failed relationships.

But, this time I was tired of it. I didn't want to keep praying the same prayer over and over again: "Lord, please forgive me for my sins," or "Lord, please bless this relationship, even though I'm not doing what I can to bless you." I didn't want to confuse yet another situation or end up being emotionally distraught because I had once again decided to make sex the foundation of our relationship. I didn't want to later look down the road and wonder if he was truly with me because he wanted to be with me or if it was only because of my "flower."

> "Note to self: Sometimes big blessings require big sacrifices."

And that was the day Eric (who would later become my husband) and I decided to become celibate.

Guess what? Sex isn't bad. All of my life I heard how bad sex was, but hardly ever did I hear just how enjoyable it can be when you're married. When I consider how God intended for sex to be originally, it's no wonder why He wanted it that way. Although we live in a society that encourages whatever whenever, I see now just why God set it up like he did.

Think about it. How much more special would it be if you and your husband could experience the first time together? How exciting would it be if you and your husband could actually experiment and try new things together versus having to accept the reality that each of you experienced something so special, but with someone else or a plethora of other people? Unfortunately, that's usually not the case and it definitely wasn't the case for my husband and I, because of what we did prior to meeting each other.

God is a God of order. While I do believe we sin against God when we do not follow His word, I also believe we can have a beautiful future despite not having such a clean past. There are plenty of stories today, and from the Bible, that provide evidence for it.

Nonetheless, when I consider the negative ramifications of sex and how the misuse of it has negatively affected so many lives, I understand more clearly why God designed it the way he did. I'm not here to argue about sex, what's permissible and what isn't, whether or not celibacy will fireproof your marriage, and so on. Instead, I'm merely here to share my personal experience of why Eric and I decided to wait and how it impacted our relationship with each other and with God.

I believe it's what we do with sex and how we perceive it and use it as a substitute for love that often causes us to make bad decisions or end up in bad relationships…at least that's how it was for me. For a period in my life, I actually believed where there was sex, there was love. It may sound ridiculous but for someone like me, who was single and yearning for a love I lacked from within and from others, the distinction of love and sex wasn't always clear for me. I used to assume sex was the end-all be-all, but it wasn't. Nor does it automatically provide the authentic, long lasting relationships we so desire.

I can't speak for everyone but I know I have ruined countless relationships or ended up with a broken heart because, somewhere along the way, I figured the presence of sex automatically meant the presence of love. Trust me, physical attraction, sex, and intimacy—they matter—especially when you're married. But physical attraction can become a major distraction if you're not careful.

I know, without a shadow of a doubt, much of my past hurt and pain was due in part because I either gave myself too soon or because I assumed he would love me because I had sex with him. Even though I knew the Lord was telling me to wait and His word says to wait, I got caught up in what I wanted and what felt good to me. I wanted to do what I wanted to do. Little did I know, at the time, that what may feel good to you may not always be good for you.

Simply put, I used to equate love with sex. I assumed the sexual exchange was his way of exchanging his heart with mine even though most times it had absolutely nothing to do with love. Don't get me wrong, God intended for sex to be a pleasant experience at the right time and between a husband a wife. So, it is totally natural to enjoy it as much we do.

I can admit, however, in the past I took advantage of it in certain situations. In my younger years, I wasn't as responsible with my sexual activities as I could have been, especially considering what I know now. Despite the fact that I wanted the attention and the affection, I still knew within myself that I could've done things differently. I can't beat myself up about it though. You live and you learn.

I remember there were times when I was so confused and so reluctant to end one relationship because I had to face the fact that, yes, I had given up so much of myself to someone who no longer wanted to be with me. My feelings were attached to the sex. That's why, a lot of times, I was so emotional. I found it difficult to move on and deal with the consequences of the break-up, because I was still dealing with the consequences of sharing my body.

There were times when I thought I could just have sex with certain guys and be okay with it, but that seldom rang true. At the time, I didn't realize just how deep my self-esteem or "daddy issues" were. I thought I was having sex for pleasure; but, I was really having sex because I thought it would help me feel better about myself and, even worse, would prove that someone loved me. My goodness, it's hard to go back to that place, even now as I'm writing, when I think about whom I opened up myself to.

To be quite honest, I engaged in sex because I thought that's what I had to do in order to get a man to like me or to get him to stay with me. I used it to confirm how much he liked me, so I thought. I actually thought I was special because of it.

I used to tell myself things like, "He could probably get it from anyone, but he chose me. I know he will not be with me if I tell him I don't want to have sex. He will think I am weird if I don't do it. I have to have sex with him to show him I am the best he has ever had." It's tough, but it's real. I used to say these things to justify why having sex was necessary for the development of our relationship.

I actually thought sex cured everything and would make a man stay no matter what. I figured since he was a man, then it was my job to supply his needs, except it wasn't my job because he wasn't my husband. I should've been more concerned about what *I* needed. I used to put purity, righteousness, and even my willingness to try on the backburner. Oftentimes, I asked God to bless my relationships and help keep us together, but I wasn't doing anything to bless Him when it came to my relationship.

It wasn't until years later that I decided to train my brain to think beyond sex. I started to really think about whether or not I knew the guy, if he was worth the time, or if he truly and genuinely cared about me. To love someone is to know someone, so I started doing a better job of getting to know the people I was with, instead of using sex as the determining factor for the relationship. And that's when Eric came into the picture.

Remaining celibate was quite difficult to do, because we were so attracted to each other. We both made the commitment. For Eric and me, something felt different about our connection. We knew that if we wanted something different, we had to do something different. We didn't want it to be like the same old, tired relationships. We wanted to show God how serious we were about making this thing work.

I will admit we started off making some of the same mistakes in the beginning and treated our relationship just like the old ones. Since he was older than I, I was convinced he wanted a woman who would supply his every, need including sex. Besides, who would think that in the twenty-first century there was a man who was willing to commit and be celibate and be faithful to me when he could go and find any other woman to have sex with? Contrary to popular belief, it was possible because, with God, anything is possible, no matter what society, the media, the TV shows, or even our friends and family say.

The more we talked and the more time we spent together, the more I realized just how different he was and even how much I had changed. At the time, I couldn't decipher whether it was just my feelings taking control or if he truly were different. There was something special about him when he spoke to me or when he was around me. He treated me like a real man is supposed to treat a real woman. It was evident to me that he was "A man of God, first before anything."

Because of our decision, we experienced something we never experienced before with anyone else: true intimacy. Both of us, not just one of us, were actively pursuing a righteous life that was pleasing to God. In the end, it made us even that much stronger knowing that we were working together with God.

What I noticed the most about all of this was the fact I no longer experienced the same issues that soured some of my past relationships. The constant paranoia, nagging, or lack of trust seemed to dissipate, because we were more concerned about feeding our spiritual desires than feeding our physical desires.

The more time we spent together, the more it became apparent how much we had prayed to find each other. Not only had God blessed us with what we *wanted*, but He blessed us with what we *needed* from each other. He blessed us with each other for a reason. Needless to say, we had to check ourselves pretty quickly. At the rate we were going, we were headed down a path that could have potentially destroyed what God intended for us had we not decided to remain celibate.

Of course I cannot take the credit and act as if it were so easy or as if it were solely my decision to become celibate. We all know the flesh likes to do what the flesh likes to do, but it was God who spoke through my pastor at that time and who pushed me to have the courage to do what was right—what I knew I was supposed to be doing.

All of my life I heard messages about not having sex before marriage and how it was a sin and so on and so on. It wasn't until my pastor did a series on sexual immorality that I changed my life. It was the first time I was convinced—and at the same time was compelled—to actually do something different. He broke it down and explained it in such a way, that it made me realize just how damaging sexual immorality was, not only physically, but spiritually, too.

He challenged us take a closer look as to why sexual immorality was so harmful to our lives and how it would prevent us from inheriting the Kingdom of God. Of course it wasn't what I wanted to hear at the time, but obviously it was what I needed to hear. Based on everything that was taking place in my life, I knew God was about to do a new thing. I realized the potential ramifications of my past actions, as well as my future ones, which included physical, emotional, and spiritual damage.

So, after weeks of trying and failing and going back and forth, we knew what we had to do. We finally made the decision to remain abstinent until the day we said our vows. This was long before we were engaged. At first it seemed like something that was impossible, because I was so into him and he was so into me. Naturally, you want to share a physical relationship with someone you really like. Clearly, we were attracted to each other. I mean, why wouldn't I want to touch and kiss his beautiful, milk chocolate skin? Why wouldn't I want to feel his strong arms wrapped around me? That was totally natural.

> "Note to self:
> We understood that if God were going to bless our union and take us to another level, then we also had to take things to another level."

However, we understood that if God were going to bless our union and take us to another level, then we also had to take things to another level. Usually people refer to the "next level" as sex, but our next level was the level of spiritual maturity. We un-derstood how con-tradictory our prayers were going to be, had we prayed and asked for Him to keep us together. So, we knew we had to position ourselves on a path to receive God's favor. We knew God had brought us together for this special moment, and we wanted the moment to last for a lifetime. Sometimes you have to sacrifice your temporary desires for permanent reward.

Eric even took it a step further and decided that, in order to help us remember our promise to God, he would seal the deal with a ring. The ring served as a symbol of our commitment and as a friendly reminder of the promise, which was necessary especially during times of weakness.

Someone may be reading this now and thinking, "I just can't do that. That's not realistic in today's world," But like I said earlier, it is possible. I understand it's not the easiest thing for people nowadays, but there are men willing to do what they need to do for the right woman. Before I met Eric, that was something neither he or I ever thought we could have done. It worked because both of us were willing to make the sacrifice.

Just think if you did, or even tried, you could very well be the catalyst that inspires and encourages others to do the same. Understand that, if and when you make the decision, there will be those who will argue that you're making the wrong decision, because they acknowledge you are raising the standard. They will remind you of how difficult it is and may try to convince you that it is not even worth the sacrifice, because maybe they don't agree or they're not ready to move out of their comfort zone. Your real friends and the ones closest to you will support you no matter what—even if you slip up—but don't let anyone keep you from the blessing you'll get out of it.

I know there were times when I missed out on certain blessings or I struggled with discerning between what was good and what was bad, because I was more concerned with pleasing my fleshly desires instead of pleasing God. Eric and I didn't want our flesh and personal desires to influence our actions. So, even when it got rough, prayer was definitely essential for us. There were times when all we could do was pray because our flesh was trying to do everything it could to control our actions.

I understand this may not be for everyone and this may not come as easily for others and I may have lost some at the beginning of the chapter. I just know, when it came time to experiencing true love, that celibacy helped eliminate a lot of confusion and we were able to make better decisions that were influenced by love more than sex.

When I think about my sexual partners and how much I sacrificed for those who didn't even stick around for more than a day, a week, or even a month, I'm grateful and thankful that things didn't turn out like they could have. I realize now I was only one sexual encounter away from a STD. I was only one sexual encounter away from dealing with baby mama drama. Hence, I'm forever grateful and thankful.

At the end of the day, we must consider the consequences of our decisions. Sometimes, you have to discern between what feels good to you and what is good for you. Thankfully, you get the best of both worlds when you experience real love. That's not always the case if you're with someone who isn't meant for you. Don't overlook future necessities just to satisfy your present desires.

Lesson Six

Make yourself a priority while you can.

My college graduation party was epic! My mom planned a wonderful evening with great food, fellowship, and entertainment. A lot of my sorority sisters were there and some of my friends even drove up from Louisville to Lexington to celebrate with me.

It was a great time. I felt so honored and blessed to know I had made it through. I was the second, after my brother, from our generation to graduate from college. So, not only was it a momentous occasion for me and my mother, but for the rest of my family as well.

But what would you think if I told you that, just a few years prior, I actually considered dropping out of school in hopes of pursuing something totally different-all because of a guy? From the surface it seemed like it was all because of the company I used to work for, but that wasn't necessarily true.

At the time, I was working with this awesome organization. There were quite a few successful people within the business, including my boyfriend at the time. I was traveling to different cities, meeting millionaires and billionaires, getting promoted to new tiers and levels. Even though I had to make an investment upfront in order to build my "network," I started making a little extra money on the side. However, it wasn't something I really wanted to do, but I tried it anyway.

In the midst of everything, I started feeling overwhelmed and that my priorities were out of order. I was juggling school, my position as a resident assistant, my extracurricular activities, my boyfriend, and our relationship. At one point I figured it was all too much and maybe college wasn't the right thing for me, even though I knew how important it was for me to finish what I started. I used the business as my scapegoat to justify my reasoning for slacking on priorities like going to church, or keeping my grades up.

Back then I figured, "I have to make money, because God wants me to be prosperous." Yes, God wanted me to live an abundant and prosperous life, but not at the expense of living without Him. Besides, to live abundantly doesn't always imply money. I spent less time studying and focused more on the business, earning extra money, and buying things I really didn't need.

I reached a point where the business wasn't going as well as when I first started. Plus, I was on college student budget, which wasn't much. I realized I was putting more into the business than I was receiving and that my clientele list wasn't growing. All of my life I dreamt of graduating with a degree, knowing I was going to be one of the few in my family to accomplish that goal. But, for some reason, I thought it would make more sense to take a break from school and concentrate solely on this new business venture. I cannot even imagine how my mom would have reacted had I told her at the time.

Needless to say, everything I contemplated had less to do with the business venture and more to do with me putting my boyfriend's priorities above everything else. I was more interested in his plans than my own. He was the one who told me I was wasting my time trying to graduate, even though I was almost finished. I supported him and his ventures, but he didn't support what I was trying to do.

Obviously, I was more concerned with his plans and what he wanted to do. In the midst of everything, I almost forgot me—all because I was too afraid of losing someone whom I wasn't meant to be with anyway.

Have you ever heard of someone with the chameleon syndrome (not be confused with napoleon syndrome)? I used to be that girl. I used to change who I was, or who I wanted to be, based on the guy I was dating at the time.

> "Note to self: Don't let your single status keep you stagnant."

For instance, if there were a certain genre of books he was into, then I read the same ones. I'd never read so many Eric Jerome Dickey books in my life (they were great, though). If my boyfriend were into a certain musical artist, then I listened to the same type of music. Whatever he was into, I tried that much harder to have the same interests.

At times I got a little lost, sacrificed my moral compass, and started going my boyfriend's direction. No matter what it was, even if I wasn't the least bit interested, I found a way to act as if I were just as interested as he. I was willing to change my direction or who I was just to cater to my boyfriend.

I was so obsessed with dating and having a boyfriend that a lot of times I forgot my own priorities. Often times I would neglect my needs merely to satisfy my wants. After going through the situation with the business venture and college and after some deep soul searching, I finally came back to my senses. I would no longer commit to someone at the expense of putting my own needs on the backburner. In other words, don't change your plans and cater to someone who isn't willing to cater to you.

Many times during my single season, I became so obsessed with finding "the one" or trying to be in a relationship, it took me awhile to figure it out one of the best lessons I learned: Don't allow your single status to keep you stagnant.

There were times when I made decisions or changed my mind about things merely because I was obsessed with someone else. I will never forget the time I went away for an internship at a well-known international company. It was the opportunity of a lifetime that could have led to even more opportunities. Even though it wasn't the ideal living situation, it was in a sunny state.

To make a long story short, I don't think I made it past a month before I was on the first flight back home to Kentucky. Why? Because I wanted to get back home to the guy I was dating at that time. Although I can admit I was homesick at times, I also know the relationship heavily influenced my decision to go back home.

That was one of the few times in my life I did something I rarely do—I quit.

I'm blessed to live the life I have now but who knows what would have happened had I stayed? I admit that many of my decisions weren't always rational, mainly because my focus wasn't always clear.

Sometimes we make everything and everyone else a priority above ourselves without even knowing it. Think about when you've experienced a difficult break-up. I used to spend so much time crying and trying to hang on. Months would go by and I still found myself focused on what happened or focused on the old situations. I would occupy my mind with negative thoughts like:

"I wonder what he's doing."

"I wonder if he's going to call."

"I'm going to make him pay for what he did to me."

"I can't believe he would do this to me after all we've been through."

"I wonder if I should call him."

"He knows he loves me and we'll be back together."

"He's just young. He'll grow up and learn and then he'll be begging for me to get back with him."

I harbored so much bitterness and frustration, not realizing my mindset affected my emotions, my actions, and even my language. Of course, I needed to take time and deal with the hurt and pain, but I wasted a lot of energy and time worrying about what did or didn't happen. I would lay in my bed, crying or depressed. I reached a point where the heartache and my unwillingness to see beyond the situation pushed me to a point where I stopped living for me, because I got so caught up living for everyone else.

Once I couldn't let go of someone for a year. Yes, that's correct—an entire year. I know some of you may have experienced similar situations for much longer. For an entire year I played mind games with myself. I nursed a false hope that he would see the light and want me back.

Part of the problem, though, was I allowed him to play mind games, which ultimately prevented me from moving on. I let him manipulate me in a way so that he did and said just enough to keep me waiting, which in turn caused me to basically put my life on hold for him while he did whatever with whomever whenever. Still, I waited and did whatever I could to remain a part of his life.

I presented a façade to my friends and those closest to me. I didn't tell them I was still thinking about him and how much I wanted him back, let alone that I was still seeing him. That was a big mistake, because sometimes we need our girlfriends to push us to move on. We need them to remind us that we have so much more to live for than a relationship, especially a failed relationship. Unfortunately, I wasn't ready to hear that I was wasting my time, which was nothing less than the truth.

At that dismal time, I thought some of the things he said were reasonable and made sense, not realizing it was all a part of his manipulation. He told me things he knew I wanted to hear, like: "Even though I'm with her, I don't care about her like I care about you. I think, eventually or one day, we could be back together. Yes, I still love you. I'll never stop loving you. I just need time to figure some things out."

Yes, I know what you're thinking. Why did I think he was going to be with me when I knew he was with someone else? Why was I willing to wait and put my life on hold for someone who wasn't willing to hold onto me?

Even though he wasn't cheating on me, because clearly I wasn't his girl per se, I later realized just how much I cheated myself. I almost kept myself from the life God had for me, because I was so obsessed with the life I thought I was supposed to have with someone else.

Nevertheless, I got tired of waiting. I don't want anyone to wait as long or even longer than I did for something or someone who isn't willing to wait for her. That was just a year for me, but I pray for my sister who's been waiting or has put her life on hold for even longer than that. Part of loving ourselves means making ourselves a priority. When you're single, that's just the right time.

.

Considering everything I went through and the decisions I made—and almost made—I'm encouraged to tell others to invest in you. Invest in your own spiritual, mental, and physical health. Invest in your career, your business, your organization, your dreams, your goals, your future, your brand. Invest in something fun, like traveling and learning new skills. Do it while you have all of the time in the world!

That's not to say that you can't do any of that when you're married, but the Bible tells us in First Corinthians 1:7: "...An unmarried woman or virgin is concerned about the Lord's affairs: Her aim is to be devoted to the Lord in both body and spirit. But a married woman is concerned about the affairs of this world—how she can please her husband...." When a woman marries, her husband becomes her main priority (and vice versa). But, regardless of whether single or married, you have to make time for you. As women, we hold a lot of titles—daughter, wife, mother, sister, entrepreneur, professional, etc. It's okay to take time out for yourself.

While you have the opportunity and the time, focus on what you can do while you're single. Don't be like me and get so caught up in someone else's life that you miss out on your own life.

My single sister, you are too beautiful, too intelligent, and too wonderful a person to waste your single life. Instead, take advantage of it and do something. Explore a new city or explore the world. Finish school. Launch that site or blog you've been talking about. Start that new business or non-profit. Start selling your handmade products on Etsy. Devote more of your time to volunteering and serving others. Find a ministry and become a part of something bigger than yourself. Take up a new hobby. Whatever it is, do you and be you!

We have to face reality and accept the fact that being single is not a curse. It's not something which we should be ashamed of; it just means you have different priorities than those who aren't. I realize now that much of my single life was really designed so I could learn and grow, which I did, but I definitely could have devoted a lot more time to my walk with Christ as well as to my own personal interests.

A lot of times I went from one guy to the next, thinking the next man was going to heal me from my past pain. I really should've been taking more advantage of my single status to get to know myself and do more for myself. Had I done that, it's possible I could have realized my purpose and God's plan for my life much sooner. I also could have avoided a lot of unnecessary scenarios; however, I also realize that my life could have turned out differently and that I may not have been able to do what I'm doing today.

Think of your single status as a blessing, not a burden. Use this time for yourself and your relationship with God so that, if and when the love of your life comes along you will have greater discernment about whom you're supposed to be with. Life is short, so remember to live it to the fullest: full of new experiences, full of passion, full of laughter, and full of fun.

.

I remember reading a story awhile back about a woman who was married for a long time. She had a husband, children, and everything.

Somewhere along the way, I guess she grew tired of it all. So, guess what she did? She packed her bags, left her husband and kids, and traveled across country to California to begin a whole new life. She did not look back and I don't think she went back. Of course once I read the story, it posed the question: "What on Earth would cause a woman to pack up and leave her family?"

While I don't encourage this type of behavior, I'm sympathetic to her plight. It can be quite difficult when you're married, managing a family, home, job, and whatever else. I'm willing to bet, at some point or another, she felt overwhelmed, frustrated, and confused; which ultimately led to her feeling like she lost herself.

Although her story falls on the extreme end of the spectrum, I have experienced situations in which it seemed as though I were losing my identity. Even worse, there were times when I did lose myself. We reach a point where we, our goals, or our aspirations no longer matter or we forget what it's like to think and do for ourselves.

It's ironic that sometimes love—or what appears to be love—finds us, but we end up losing ourselves. Throughout the years, however, I've learned how to avoid losing myself in love and would like to share a few tips with you, based on what's worked for me, even now as a married woman.

How to Avoid Losing Yourself in Love

Always keep God first. I used to be so caught up in the madness of love that I was more concerned about pleasing others instead of God. Now, as a married woman and despite how much I love and adore my husband, I can't neglect my relationship with God. I understand now, more than ever, there is no us without Him. Not only is God a priority for me, but He's a priority for my husband as well. Stop neglecting the relationship you need the most just so you can have the relationship you want.

Get a life and let him have one too. I'm not the type who refuses to let her man out of her sight for more than five seconds. Trust me, Eric and I love spending time with each other, but we also enjoy spending time with our friends. Just because we enjoy spending time with our friends doesn't mean we love each other any less. We have a partnership that's built on trust, honesty, communication, and mutual understanding and respect.

> **"Note to self: Be the woman a man needs, not a needy woman."**

So, I can have my "girls' night out" when I need it and he can hang out with the "fellas" when he needs to. Furthermore, even though we have two totally different careers and aspirations, I can pursue my goals and passions while he pursues his. We support each other.

Be the woman a man needs, not a needy woman. While most men want to feel needed, they don't want a woman who is so desperately dependent on them that she can't stand on her own two feet. On those days when my husband has dealt with more than his fair share of life's burdens, he needs to know I can be just as strong and supportive for him as he is for me.

Don't always succumb to the pressure. People like for you to do what they want you to do, but don't fall into the trap. Whether single or married, you can pretty much guess how the line of questioning will go. If you're single, everyone asks about a boyfriend. When you get a boyfriend, they ask when are you getting married. When you get married, they ask when is the baby coming. Before the baby turns three months old, they want to know when the second baby is coming. I couldn't stop people from asking those questions, but I stopped feeling like I had to do things based on what other people expected me to do.

Every marriage and relationship is different. Everyone is on a different life journey when it comes to careers and life changes. I learned it was okay to say, "I want to do X, Y, and Z first," or "I want to wait until…"

What's most important is that my husband and I have open communication, so we can make the best decisions together based on what's best of us—not everyone else. You have to do the same with your own life and do what's best for you.

Squeeze in some "me" time. Because of our natural tendency, as women, to love and help nurture the lives of others—our men, our children, our friends, our family/loved ones—it's easy to forget to take care of ourselves. I'll be the first to admit, I live for a good calendar, checklist, and task list, but sometimes I give and give until I have nothing left to give or until my body physically shuts down.

While my main purpose here on Earth is to serve God and His people, how useful can I really be if I lack the spiritual, mental, and physical nourishment I need to keep going? I have learned that sometimes saying "no" to everyone else means saying "yes" to yourself.

I used to struggle with saying "no"—and still do sometimes—but my husband has helped me with this. He reminds me that I can't be everything to everybody. The fact that other people don't have a problem saying "no" when they need to should encourage me to do it even more.

My mom always reminds me, "You can't be at two places at one time." So, at times, I've had to say "no" to certain people, not necessarily because I wanted to, but in most cases because I had to. Just like the safety instructions on an airplane tell us, "Put on your oxygen mask first before you begin helping others." It's not about being selfish; rather it's about being the best I can be to and for myself so I can be the best to and for everyone else.

Sometimes it's as simple as going to Target or staying home alone while Eric goes out and enjoys happy hour with his boys. Whether it's a massage, retail therapy, going for a walk, taking a workout class, reading, writing, or just having some quiet time, I always try to make time for myself. I think First Lady Michelle Obama summed it up best when she said: "Women in particular need to keep an eye on their physical and mental health; because, if we're scurrying to and from appointments and errands, we don't have a lot of time to take care of ourselves. We need to do a better job of putting ourselves higher on our own 'to do' list."

Be willing to compromise, as long as it doesn't compromise who you are. One of the things I love so much about my husband is that he allows me to be myself, despite how different we are. While I love being my husband's wife and I love being married, I also love being who God created me to be and carrying out God's plans for my life.

Compromise is especially important when it comes to marriage and relationships, but it doesn't work if only one person is willing to compromise. You don't have to settle for someone and sacrifice what you believe merely for the sake of being with someone. The one who truly loves you will love you for you and won't make you choose between what is right or wrong, based on his or her own selfish desires or motives.

―――――――

This is all to say: don't get so wrapped up in someone else's life so much so that you neglect your own life. Stop waiting for him to leave her. Stop waiting for him to make the relationship public. Stop waiting for him to grow up or make a decision. It's not fair for you to wait on someone else, while he's busy running the streets. Take back your power. Remember to be you and do you. I'm a living witness that you can have love and still have a life, too.

Lesson Seven

Don't make excuses for people who need to be excused from your life.

It was a nice, warm, and sunny day, and I was smiling from ear to ear. The bright rays of sunlight shined even brighter as they hit against my ring.

I was newly engaged and enjoying every minute of it. I felt so honored that Eric chose me to spend the rest of his life with him and I couldn't wait! Then, my phone rang. I didn't recognize the number, but I answered it anyway:

"Hello?"

"Hey, girl. What's up?"

"Oh hey," I responded reluctantly. "Is this who I think it is?"

"Yeah, it's me. How you been? How's everything going?"

"Oh, I'm doing great! Life is good and I couldn't be any happier."

"Yeah, I bet," he replied. "I heard you're engaged now."

"Yes, I am. I'm really excited. He is definitely a great guy and unlike anyone I have ever met before."

"That's what's up. I'm really happy for you."

"Well, thank you. I appreciate it. So, what's up? Why'd you call me?"

"Is this a good time to talk? I just had to get something off my chest."

"Yeah, I guess but I only have a few moments. What's up?"

"Look, Shonda, I just wanted to apologize to you for any and everything I ever did to hurt you. I started thinking about when we used to date and how much fun we had, and I just want to let you know you really were a great girlfriend. Even though I am really happy for you, I can't help but to think back and realize how great a girl I had. I don't want to be disrespectful or anything, but I just wanted to let you know I'm sorry for what I did and how I treated you. I am different now and I don't know what would have happened with us, but I just want to say I am sorry and I hope we can be cool."

I was shocked, yet unmoved.

"Uh, thanks but I'm good," I responded. "I appreciate your apology, but, quite honestly, I have moved on and there really wasn't any reason for you to apologize. I hadn't even really thought about that stuff in a long time and it doesn't bother me, so it's all water under the bridge. I'm over it. It is what it is, but I'm good and I don't really think there's a need for us to continue talking or to continue a friendship. What's done is done and I've moved on from all of that, but I appreciate you calling."

———

That was just one of many calls and texts I received from that ex-boyfriend, and others, when I first got engaged. The funny thing is, that call took place roughly six to seven years after the time he and I first started dating.

———

"He just needs time."

"I don't want to be mean."

"I'm afraid what his life will be like without me in it."

"He needs me, and I think I can help him be the man he needs to be."

"I know it's been awhile, but we have a long history."

Excuses, excuses, excuses—these are just some of the things we tell ourselves

> "Note to self: Say "no" to people who make more withdrawals than deposits."

to keep people around for longer than necessary even if it's not good for us.

When I received that phone call, I could have easily made an excuse for this ex. I could have told myself he was a nice guy and there was no harm in being friends. However, I knew, deep down inside, his intentions weren't pure.

There's an old saying: "You never know what you got until its gone." It is interesting when you break up with someone, then get a new man, get engaged, or get married. It's like Batman's signal goes out to your exes and they find out, either through social media or the rumor mill. Then, somehow, they find a way to get in contact with you. Most times it's really just to see if the window of opportunity is still open and if there's still room for them to slide back in. Don't fall for it. Although this particular ex-boyfriend was polite, respectful, and apologetic when he called, I was not trying to go back. I was reading a different book and starting a new chapter in my life.

I understand some people do in fact try to make a mends with people they've hurt in the past; but, I was not willing to take a chance and potentially open up a new can of worms…or should I say old can of worms. I didn't want him to think for one second that, even if he thought he had a chance to be a part of my life, that I was going to let him slip back in.

He thought he was talking to the same young, naïve Shonda he'd known, but I was a different person. I was no longer interested in making excuses for people who needed to be excused from my life. I was a grown woman with a new man in my life. I was no longer concerned about what had happened. I was more focused on what was happening and what was about to happen.

If people hinder you more than they help you, then it's time to move on. If they make more withdrawals than deposits, then they're draining you. As I've dealt with past relationships and ex-boyfriends, I've observed mainly two types of people we often deal with: deadweight and pop-ups.

"Deadweights" are people who like to stay around, but they constantly mistreat you or bring you down. They're like the baggage that weighs you down because of old issues or constant drama. I used to be what Erykah Badu referred to as the "bag lady." I was that girl. I used to carry around my emotional baggage from one relationship to the next, and would leave with even more baggage. I'd leave one and carry the bitterness, anger, resentment, and everything else over to the next one.

If I was dating a guy and he did something extremely hurtful or caused an immeasurable amount of pain, I still found a way to go back to him or keep him around for longer than I should have. If I started dating a new guy, I was consumed with what happened in the past and would sometimes unknowingly treat the new guy like one of those past boyfriends. I inadvertently made them pay for past mistakes committed by others. I failed to realize I was emotionally unavailable. I was incapable of moving on to something better, because I hadn't let go of the other relationship. Eventually, I realized it was time to drop the baggage. I could no longer carry around the dead weight of relationships. Plus, no one carries his or her luggage around all of the time anyway.

In addition to deadweight, there are the "pop-ups." Pop-ups are those who run in and out of your life when it's convenient for them, but they are never consistent. The only thing consistent about them is their inconsistency. They come, they go, they come back again, and then they leave again. The one from the story at the beginning of the chapter—he was a classic example of a pop-up. There were other cases too.

Pop-ups like to call and text every now and then, just to make sure we're still thinking about them. They do just enough to keep the door cracked open. Sometimes we hear from them and sometimes we don't. They convince us to wait on them, while they do what they want to do. They're the ones who date us only in private, but expect us to date them exclusively. Pop-ups tell us to wait, but show no signs of forward progression; nor do they provide any signs of hope for a future with real commitment.

We spend countless days, months, and even years dealing with pop-ups. Instead of making a decision to move forward, we settle and choose to wait. Sometimes we keep certain people around or stay in relationships "just because," but comfort and convenience aren't substitutes for love. Although it's nice to have someone around, we can't use comfort and convenience as excuses to stay in relationships or be around people who may not be good for us.

For me, being comfortable meant staying with someone merely because of how long I knew him or because he made me feel comfortable when he was around, even if that meant he treated me like crap. Comfort meant I stayed with certain people, even though I knew the relationship was going nowhere and nothing positive was coming from it.

On the other hand, convenience meant there was someone I could call if I needed to talk or if I wanted him to come over for whatever reason. Even though we may not have been together and even though I knew he didn't want to necessarily be with me (or vice versa), it was convenient to have him around to keep me company.

Instead of allowing deadweight and pop-ups to keep us running in circles and confused, sometimes we have to come up with creative ideas to help us move on or get rid of them. Whether that means deleting them as friends on Facebook, blocking them on our phones or social media pages, changing our numbers…we have to do what we have to do. I've had to use the "block" and "delete" functions on my phone to ensure I didn't keep falling back into the trap of answering their calls or responding to their text messages. Sometimes you have to take extreme measures when you know you can't trust yourself. Plus, it serves as a sign to yourself and everyone else just how committed you are to moving on.

I had moments when I debated with myself whether or not I should call. I would make a declaration and tell myself that if he called, then I wouldn't answer. Then, as soon as his number would appear on my phone, I would fall back into the trap.

I used to hate when I would go out unexpectedly and run into my ex-boyfriend, or see him with another girl. That's why I had to take extreme measures to make sure I didn't end up going

.

back to the same situation from which I had once been delivered. The last thing you want is to stay bound to something from your past that could potentially keep you from your future.

Have you ever eaten at a restaurant and noticed how the waiters use certain doors to enter and return to the kitchen? On a few occasions, I've observed waiters attempting to enter through the door intended for exit and crash into those trying to exit. With food, beverages and everything in hand, it all goes tumbling down.

That's how it is when it comes to letting go of certain people. It's a friendly reminder as to why we have signs that read "enter" or "exit." Exit is the opposite of entrance. It reminds us why it's not always possible to enter into dimensions or new levels of our lives with our exes attached.

Any experienced driver understands we cannot focus our eyes solely on the rear view mirror while driving. If we did, we wouldn't be able to fully focus on the view through the windshield and pay attention to what's coming ahead.

The same is true with our own lives: we can't move forward if we're focused on the rear view mirror of our painful pasts. Instead, we must pay attention to the beautiful windshields of our future. In order to reach your desired destination, the very first thing you have to do is actually leave your current location.

Furthermore, we have to be open and honest with ourselves. I had a friend tell me one day, "I really do want him out of my life."

I told her, "No, you don't. Just be honest. Because if you did, then you would make it so." If we're constantly going back and forth between our exes or constantly making excuses for them, it's quite possible the door hasn't been fully closed. If it's easy for them to step in and out whenever they feel like it, then obviously we're not quite ready to let go.

> *"Note to self: We can't move forward if we're focused on the rear view mirror of our painful pasts."*

However, by doing this, it causes us to potentially miss out on what's around the corner. When we finally decide to close those chapters in our lives, we have to firmly decide and commit to doing just that even if that means enlisting the help of family and friends. It's okay to say we're not ready to move on, but we have to be real with ourselves.

Sometimes, a sure sign we haven't truly let go is often reflected in how we act or how we treat our new significant others. Sometimes we don't even realize how we are treating our new men until they finally tell us or we reflect back on some of our own personal mistakes. I used to get caught up in what used to be instead of accepting and appreciating how things were supposed to be.

At times, we resist the right things and accept the wrong things. We spend so much time thinking about the exes and neglect the new men in our lives. We have to release the pain of our past and be open to new and better things.

Anyone who knows me knows how big of a fan I am of Beyonce. There's one particular song of hers titled *Best Thing I Never Had*. In the video, you witness her sincere desire for another guy who is the least bit interested in her. Later in life, you see her getting married to someone else, and she realizes that what she once thought she wanted actually wasn't the best thing for her at the time. Eventually she says, "Thank God I found the good in goodbye."

That's my favorite part of the song! I don't know about you but there's a liberating feeling knowing what you once thought was the best thing in your life became the best thing when it was actually removed from your life. Even though we experience bad situations, we can still find the good in goodbye.

I'll never forget when I went through a terrible break-up after discovering that my boyfriend had been cheating on me. I was so hurt and distraught that I actually called my mom crying and sobbing and told her, "I'm sorry for not always listening and for not always taking your advice." I couldn't stop crying for what seemed like forever. I was so depressed that one day I literally quit my job, drove home to my mom's house and stayed there for about a week.

Aside from relationships and "puppy love," there was another time a few short years ago when I was dealing with a difficult situation as it related to my career. My work environment was toxic and I found myself dealing with extreme anxiety, so much so that I had what I believed to be a panic attack. I was also going through so much in my own personal life and dealing with grief.

I finally decided to make a move. I decided I had to get out of that toxic environment. My boss offered me a promotion with a significant pay increase, but I turned it down. I basically said, "Bye, Felicia," and accepted a new position with a different company, making a lateral move instead. Some people thought I was crazy for turning down the promotion and salary increase; but, for me at that time, peace of mind was more important than the number of zeroes on my paycheck.

What's interesting now is when I look back at those dark times in my life and I realize what I once thought I wanted was exactly what I didn't need. Sometimes we struggle with moving forward, because all we see is what we left behind versus what lies ahead.

We're so focused on what we lost instead of what we look to gain, that sometimes the very thing we hold onto is the very thing that holds us back. It's hard when things end. There's always something new, but that "something better" isn't always a surety. I have learned how to find the good in goodbye by doing the following:

G – Get out of the way and let God do His thing.

How many times have we tried to do things our own way, ignored God's plans, and then complained to Him because things didn't go as we planned? It's okay to make plans for our lives, because, like they say, "If you don't plan, you plan to fail." However, conflict arises when we try to play God and orchestrate things without consulting Him, or even after talking with Him.

I don't know how many times I've prayed for God to send me a sign and remove certain people, places, or things from my life that would hinder my growth. Then, as soon as it happened, I would make excuses or I would avoid the signs because, deep down inside, that wasn't what I wanted. Sometimes we pray "Lord, send me a sign," when we really need to pray, "Lord, help me to accept it and follow through, even if the sign is different from what I wanted."

Now I know it's not about what we want, but what we need. Just like from my story earlier, I wanted so badly to be with a certain someone, despite how poorly he treated me when it was clear he didn't want to be with me.

At the end of the day, God knows just what we need when we need it. There's an old saying, be God or let God, which means either get out of the way and let God do it, or keep trying to force things to happen. We can repeatedly and hopelessly try to create the life we want by manufacturing defective relationships; or, we can hand over control to God and let Him guide and lead us so that He can make room for what we really need.

O – Open your heart and mind to something greater.

Just because something ended doesn't mean we won't have the chance to experience something better. Greater is coming.

We just have to believe it, even if that simply means greater in terms of our overall mental and spiritual capacity. I'm a better me, or will be, now that it's over. Every now and then, certain things have to end in order for something bigger and better to begin.

Yes, it's hard when things go awry or relationships end. We have to take a moment to deal with the pain and have a good cry, but we can't stay there forever. We have to pick ourselves up and keep moving.

Had I stayed crying and complaining over my failed relationships, I never would have been open and available to receive my husband's love. Had I not said goodbye to them, I wouldn't have been able to say hello to him—my husband. Had I settled for convenience, chaos, and toxic environments, I never would have stepped out on faith and fought for something better.

Sometimes we have to let go of things from our past in order to grab hold of something new. When we finally stop wasting time with "Mr. Can't Get Right," it opens up room for "Mr. Right." A good man can't occupy space in your life if it's already occupied by someone else.

Moreover, just because you haven't met "Mr. Right" doesn't mean it will never happen. Just because you hear "no" ten times doesn't mean you'll never hear a "yes."

I'll never forget when my husband was laid off during our first year of marriage. Even though it was a tough time, he *never* gave up. He always believed there was something greater coming, not only for him, but for us as a family. Everything he believed would happen for us has come to fruition. When things don't necessarily go as planned, we have to trust that God is still at work and that He can bless us with something greater. We have to put our hope in Him, not in man.

O - Observe the greater purpose and focus on what's important. I truly believe we all have a purpose, and at times, the culmination of one thing can lead to the birth of so many more things, not only in our lives but also in the lives of others. What's more encouraging than being able to help or encourage someone who is going through something you've already overcome?

That's why I do what I do. That's why I write what I write. I understand now, more than ever, that all of the so-called break-ups, disappointments, and failures I experienced in the past actually prepared me for this moment—to help someone else who may be going through similar situations. Our tests form our testimonies.

Sometimes I have to ask myself, "What is my attitude in adversity?" I realize others may be watching, and my actions and reactions can influence how they will deal with life's interruptions. So, when things get difficult, when I get discouraged and can't see clearly the good in goodbye at that moment, above all I have to remember my purpose so I can keep going.

D – Declare the victory! It's funny when we experience break-ups, heartache, or we hear the words "goodbye" or "no," we immediately find ourselves crying and focused more on what could have been instead of what could be. As human beings, it's totally natural to feel defeated and disappointed. We live, we love, we laugh, and, unfortunately, we hurt.

But how often do we take the time to rejoice about the potential catastrophes we avoided? It only takes me a second to think about where I could have been had I taken that position or had I stayed with "Tom," "Joe," or "Keith." Think about how much you could be going through right now had you stayed a little longer or had they not walked away?

Steve Maraboli once said, "As I look back on my life, I realize that every time I thought I was being rejected from something good, I was actually being re-directed to something better." Sometimes, running from God will cause us to run into the wrong things, but I thank Him for protecting us anyway.

I thank God for giving me the strength to walk away, even when I really wanted to stay. I thank God for removing certain people or things from my life that I didn't have the strength to refuse. God knew what I needed to relinquish. What's even more awesome is He knew what I stood to gain once I said goodbye. God loves us so much that, even when we think we don't need or we refuse His help, He still finds a way to help bring us out of it.

So, when I say "Thank God, I found the good in goodbye," that's just a modern way of saying what Joseph said in the Bible, "You intended to harm me, but God intended it for good" (Genesis: 50:20 NIV).

If you're not familiar with the story, Joseph said this very statement to the people who at one time considered killing him— his very own brothers. I guess they realized just how harsh that would have been, so they decided to abandon him in the desert land with the hope that he'd be sold into slavery. Just think how difficult this would have been for us to say had our own siblings plotted against us.

They did that merely because they were jealous of him. Even though they worked hard to make it happen, God had another plan for Joseph. Eventually, God made it so that Joseph was placed in a high position in the king's palace. Despite all of the plots and destructive schemes, he still came out on top because everything they meant for evil, God made it for good.

So, every broken heart, every broken relationship, every person who tried to ruin my life...it was all meant for my good. Even though I had to say goodbye to certain people and even though certain things ended, I am a better woman because of it. There is purpose in your pain and power in your purpose.

> "Note to self: I'm thankful to God for the open doors and even the ones He closed that I tried to keep open."

Like I said earlier, there is a liberating feeling knowing what you used to desperately desire ended up being something you could actually live without. Everything runs its course. If certain things and situations had not ended when they did, they could have very well prevented us from living life to our fullest potential. That's the victory!

I'm thankful to God for each and every blessing—the ones I prayed for and the ones I didn't know I needed, the open doors and even the ones He closed that I tried to keep open.

I'm reminded of this popular meme that shows a little girl holding a really small teddy bear and God holding an even bigger teddy bear. At the top of the meme, you see the words, "Trust God." We have to trust that God can create blessings out of burdens. He is waiting to bless us with more. Stop wasting time trying to make time for someone who isn't making time for you.

We can't be afraid to move on. Just because someone started with you doesn't mean he or she will finish with you. One thing about my husband, if someone crosses him or if he ends a relationship with someone, there is no going back. He has definitely helped me move past situations or relationships that ended for whatever reason.

I know now that it's okay for people to walk away. When people walk away from you, sometimes they aren't saying "no" to you; rather, they're saying no to themselves because they're not ready to step up to the level where they know they should be.

I've learned that it was never truly a loss, because you can't lose something you never really had. So, consider it just as much a blessing when people walk away, because, ultimately, they could be keeping you from a world of pain and disappointment. You have to meet people where they are and, sometimes, you have to to leave them there.

Lesson Eight

Don't be a wife to a boyfriend.

One day I got an email from a girl who needed some advice. She was dating a guy and was really into him. They had a great connection and awesome chemistry and did fun things together. Even though they lived in different cities, the distance didn't stop them from seeing each other. He was into her and she was into him.

Because she was so nice and nurturing, it was natural for her to cook and clean up his place whenever she visited him. They were like a perfect match because things were going so well. So, it was somewhat of a surprise when the relationship ended. What happened? Why did they break up when they appeared to be so great together?

She had what Oprah Winfrey likes to call an "aha moment." She realized she was the only one putting forth an effort. She was doing all of the work.

Yes, they were seeing each other and having fun, but she was the one flying across the country to make it happen. Her boyfriend never purchased an airline or train ticket so he could go see her. She re-arranged her life and her schedule to make sure they saw each other. She sacrificed her time, money, and resources to accommodate him and his needs, all while giving up her love.

Quite naturally, she started feeling as if he were taking advantage of her kindness, considering the fact she did all of the work. She made the relationship so comfortable and so convenient for him, that she almost forgot about her own needs.

> **"Note to self: Stop doing anything and everything for someone who isn't willing to do the same for you."**

Soon, it became clear the relationship wasn't going any further; nor was he willing to step up to the plate and do his part. It was like the old saying, "Why buy the cow when you can get the milk for free?" He didn't have a reason to commit to her completely, because he had practically everything he wanted without the commitment. It was clear to her that, even though he was just her boyfriend, he was reaping the benefits of a husband.

Hear me when I say this: Just because you treat a boyfriend like a husband doesn't mean he will never marry you; and, just because you don't treat him like a husband doesn't mean he will marry you. To each its own.

Nevertheless, I do believe there are certain things you can do as a girlfriend to help show your boyfriend what he can expect from you as a wife, but only if it's mutual and only if he really seems like someone with whom you could truthfully and honestly see yourself in the long term. Did I do special things for my husband when he was my boyfriend? Absolutely. Did he do things for me as his girlfriend? Absolutely, but that wasn't always the case for me. I was more like the girl in the story above.

I can't speak for everyone or every relationship, but all I know is I spent a lot of time doing anything and everything for guys who weren't willing to do anything for me. I treated my boyfriends more like husbands, even though at times I was being treated like something much less.

I used to make some of my ex-boyfriends more of a priority than anything else. If the phone rang, I answered. If they needed something, I dropped everything. I wanted to show them what they could have with a future wife like me.

There were times when I spent so much time doing things for them that I missed out on other things. Instead of studying longer, I stayed cuddled up next to them. Instead of being productive and following my own dreams, I followed theirs. Instead of making time for my friends and family, I catered more to their schedule and what they wanted to do. Similar to what I

.

discussed in an earlier chapter, I sacrificed a lot of my life and put a lot of things on hold for people who weren't the least bit concerned with holding onto me.

One day, I was asked the question, "What does it mean to make a man work for your love?" In my mind, and based on the conversations I've had with my husband, making a man work is not at all about controlling or forcing him to be with you. It's not about making him do something he doesn't want to do. As I mentioned before, that doesn't work.

Instead, it's about communicating clear and reasonable expectations from the beginning and choosing to be with men who are ready and willing to put in the effort. It's about being with men who are no longer interested in playing childish games. It all boils down to two words: *Man up!*

In other words, a man has made the conscious decision to put in the work for the right woman at the right time. That means not everyone whom we come into contact with is the right guy. Sometimes the timing just isn't right. Everyone reaches this phase at different moments in his or her life. So, not every man we run into will be ready to take this step. If only I had grasped that sooner during my single season.

I spent a lot of time doing more than enough for guys I was merely dating, thinking they would do just as much or more for me as long as I gave them what they needed. Later, I realized that, when the timing was right and the people were just right for each other, both would be willing to go above and beyond to show how serious they were about the relationship—not just any relationship, but a meaningful relationship built on love, trust, communication, compromise, and mutual respect.

A lot of married men I've talked to, including my husband, told me they wanted a challenge when it came time to settle down. They admitted they didn't really put in the effort with those whom they weren't as interested in, but they appreciated the women who made them work for it…and I'm not just talking about sex. They treasured the women who made them work for their love, appreciation, and respect, because they didn't mind working hard for the right woman. It's hard to believe nowadays, considering how it seems the "sidepieces" are winning, but just like all women can't be grouped into one bucket, neither can men.

A man earns his love from a woman based on the effort he puts into it. Considering it's the twenty-first century and people live for texting and social media (myself included—I love texting), it's no wonder the idea of courting seems like an ancient tradition.

Call me old school or traditional, but just because something is trendy and modern doesn't always mean it's the best or most effective method. I know it's 2016, and I'm not opposed to women who aren't afraid to walk up and approach a man. I personally think online dating is pretty cool. To me, it's just another place where you can meet people. At times, you're more susceptible at being lured into a relationship by means of a fictitious online persona (i.e., "cat-fished"), but I know it's worked for a lot of couples. However, I don't believe it is too much to expect a man to proactively pursue a woman and let her know how interested he is by his actions.

While technology helps us be more efficient with some of the personal and professional areas of our lives, it shouldn't be the the number one or only option when it comes to dating. It's funny when I ask single women, "When was the last time you went on a date or were actually courted by a man?" Nine times out of ten, most of them hardly even know what a real date, let alone courting, means. For many, it's been so long that they barely remember.

It's difficult to find men, let alone women, who fully understand courtship and what it means to have a man who wants to prove his love and show how interested he is in you. You can date anyone and you can even date multiple people at the same time, but it's during the courting stages that you really get to know a person on a deeper level and when you find out just how serious the other person is about the relationship.

I used to think dating was the same as courting, until my husband and some of his friends reminded me that dating leads to courtship and courtship leads to marriage. Dating is the means by which we narrow down the options, but courtship is reserved for that extra special someone who's worthy of the time and effort. Courting is like investing in a home. You may have to invest a bit more upfront in order to get and keep something that will last and eventually yield innumerable and priceless benefits.

Gone are the days when a gentleman would call a lady, ask her out, take her on a date, open the doors for her, pay for the date, and continue putting his best foot forward in an attempt to win her over. Contrary to popular belief, texting is not, and should not be, the single indicator that determines the status or magnitude of the relationship. Nor does it count as courting.

A text message on Facebook is not a replacement for picking up the phone and calling to ask someone out. A poke on Facebook or a "like" on Instagram isn't a clear sign of flirting or the most effective way to show someone you're interested. Flowers and candy emojis aren't replacements for real-life flowers and candy. "Netflix and chill" isn't a substitute for activities that actually require some thought and effort. I've learned through the years that anything worth having and keeping is worth spending some effort on…especially a good woman like me or you.

When we know better, we do better. When we expect more, we receive more. Sometimes we don't realize how bad it was (or what we were missing) until we experience the real thing. When Eric was courting me, I realized just how little I had expected from my past boyfriends. It was clear to me that I didn't require as much from others, because I didn't value myself as much. I didn't think I was worth the effort. I was too concerned about what I could do to make someone else love me or be with me, instead of acknowledging how much I was bringing to the table.

I was the prize. I had to remind myself that I was the one the Bible talked about when it said, "He who finds a wife finds a good thing" (Proverbs 18:22). I was the good thing. I was a good woman. The problem was I didn't always tell myself or believe that I was. The mistakes of my past and the lack of my father's love and effort subconsciously made me feel as if I weren't worth the effort.

So, for the woman who is reading this and wondering if she's worth it all, guess what? You are! Tell yourself, "I am that good woman. Not because of what is between my legs, but because the Word says 'I am fearfully and wonderfully made'" (Psalm 139:14).

Eric will tell you: he had to put in some extra effort in order to woo me. When we first started dating, he realized early just how different things were going to be. At the time, he was still talking to a few ladies, so there was a little overlap, as some would say.

Then, he decided he wanted to take things to the next level. He knew I wasn't willing to play "second fiddle" to another woman. I clearly communicated to him how I was not the least bit interested in playing games or dealing with nonsense. He kept telling me he wanted us to be together, but I needed his actions to match his words. There was a time when manipulation and "pillow talk" were enough for me, but that time was different.

I ended up telling him, "Get your life together." He will tell you I did. This was way before Tamar Braxton coined the now popular phrase, "Get yo life!" We still joke about it. I wasn't nasty about it or anything, but I was firm and he knew I was serious. Shortly thereafter, it was like Andre 3000 when he said in *International Players Anthem (I Choose You)* that he texted the ladies he used to talk to because he was serious about this new relationship.

And that's pretty much how it went down.

When Eric knew he was ready to be exclusive with me, he sent a text around letting those girls know. He went as far as to call and text every girl with whom he was currently or had been involved and told them he was with someone. I didn't know he did this until later on in the relationship. It was something he did on his own.

Now, initially that didn't stop the former girlfriends or "friends with benefits" immediately, but they eventually got the message, especially when he changed his number. He knew I wasn't going to settle as the "sidepiece" and I knew I deserved better.

Nonetheless, had I been okay with accepting the bare minimum, he might not have worked as hard to keep me. It was one of the first signs that proved to me how serious he was about our relationship. It was the first time I was serious about what I expected. That time I meant what I said.

Please understand, not everyone is as vocal or outspoken as I. Nor would I recommend that specific method to everyone. I was able to vocalize my expectations and stand behind them, because I was finally at a place in my life where I knew what I wanted and had a clear vision of what I expected. I knew what I wasn't going to put up with or do this time around, because, remember, I told myself, "Never again."

There is absolutely nothing wrong with wanting to do things for our men and making them feel special, whether dating or married—and especially as married women. I'm always trying to do something special for my man, even more so now because he is, in fact, my husband.

Unfortunately, however, some of us women make it so easy for men that, in turn, we make it harder for women who refuse to settle for less than what we deserve. We give it up so easily (whatever "it" may be physically, emotionally, mentally, financially, etc.) or require so little in return, that some men are immediately turned off by those of us who aren't willing to compromise our reasonable standards.

I've seen so many of us treat our so-called boyfriends like husbands who really weren't even our boyfriends. Some of them were actually husbands to other women. What good is it to give up so much of yourself to someone who hasn't the commitment to give up anything for you? That's what I mean when I say, "Don't be a wife to a boyfriend."

I was guilty of not requiring more from certain men I used to date. In the past, I tried to do everything in my power to please and keep a man, even when they didn't put in half the effort that I did. I constantly sacrificed so much of myself, but didn't expect, let alone require, the same in return. I gave up so much of myself to people who didn't deserve it. I reached a point where I was fed up. The more I learned about myself, the more I realized I needed to make a man work for my love instead of giving up everything—mind, body and soul—in return for nothing.

For some of us, it's natural to want to take care of our boyfriends and show them how good of a wife we could be, but relationships are 100/100, not 50/50. Each person has to contribute 100 percent of himself or herself and put in 100 percent effort when it comes to being the best man or woman for the other person.

I gave myself, but it wasn't reciprocated. In the end, they benefited the most while I ended up with heartache and disappointment. I think Lauryn Hill said it best with her song, *Ex-Factor*. I can't speak for anyone else, but I definitely could relate to Hill. I've been there and had to ask myself, "Who do I have to be to get some reciprocity," only to realize later I can only be me.

> "Note to self: Gone were the days when I would settle for mediocre just to say I had a man."

Just like Hill alluded to in the song, we know when something's not working. Usually someone has stopped putting in the effort or someone is putting more into the relationship than the other person. When I fell in love with my husband, I finally realized I didn't have to try to change who I was to get him to love me. I wasn't going to be the only one putting in the effort. He reminded me and showed me that real men reciprocate real love.

Gone were the days when I would settle for mediocre just to say I had a man. I had to be smarter about my choices. I had to be smarter about love. If there was ever a question of, "How do I know if he loves me," then I could respond with something more than just, "Because he told me."

Gone were the days when repeated cheating, games, and lies were acceptable. I used to tell myself and others, "I'm not putting up with this. I deserve better," or "You shouldn't put up with that. You deserve better." But then I would do exactly that—put up with the nonsense. Needless to say, I made up my mind that I would no longer accept the bare minimum or rely on words alone to prove whether or not my husband was in love with me. He proved it with his actions.

This time around, he was the initiator more often than not, which ultimately showed me two things: he was into me and he was willing to put in the work. He showed me what it really felt like to experience true love. I felt what it was to be treated like I deserved. He was constantly calling, emailing, writing letters, and texting—and vice versa. It was the opposite from the days when I was the one blowing up the phone and constantly worried about whether or not he was going to call me.

He took me out on dates and he opened doors for me. To this day, he still does the same. Eric reminded me of what courting and a real relationship looked like. He made a point to come and see me every month during the nine months we dated long-distance. This time around, I was with a man whose actions matched his words, which, in turn, helped build my confidence in him as well as our relationship. It was something I had never experienced with any other man before.

Despite all of Eric's efforts, he never felt like I wasn't into him just because he had to earn my love. He didn't have to guess what kind of wife I would be, because I was still giving him snippets of that. But this time we were all in. He knew how much I loved him; but, instead of me making all of the effort, he was willing to put in the work as well. I let him take the lead. It was a mutual relationship, versus the type where one person does more than the other.

It's been said that the woman you really want is usually the one you have to work for the most. This time, I was ready for more and I expected more, not only from him but also from and for myself as well.

Everyone has his or her own definition of what "putting in work" means and this is what it meant for me. Sometimes we have to look within ourselves and analyze our relationships based on what we want, what we need, and what we deserve. We have to ask ourselves, "Am I truly getting what I deserve? Am I being treated how a Godly woman deserves to be treated?"

Ask yourself: What do his actions say about how he feels about you? If a guy isn't willing to put in the work, then he's basically telling you you're not worth the effort. When we allow others to treat us below our standards and expectations, we also tell ourselves we're not worth it. At the end of the day, no one— male or female—should feel like he or she is doing all of the work in a relationship.

Lesson Nine

Don't be that girl—over thirty and worried.

There I was, preparing for the rollercoaster ride of my life. I walked very slowly and started wondering what had I got myself into as I approached the ride. Why did I like to live life on the edge? Was I really ready to go to the next level? Was I really ready to take a risk by getting on this ride?

A little time passed. All I could think about was my life leading up to this point and the life that was ahead of me. Had I done everything I said I wanted to do? Had I accomplished what I set out to accomplish? Why was I thinking about all of this now? What if I got on the ride and fell off? What if we did a loop and I fell out of the seat and died? I wasn't sure if I were ready for this, but I didn't really have a choice. It was time.

So, I strapped on the seatbelt and looked at the others around me. I wondered what they were thinking and compared my life to theirs. Why didn't I look like them? Why didn't I have what they had? I finally stopped focusing on the others and turned the focus back on myself.

Slowly but surely, the ride started. It was smooth sailing at first. Then a few moments later, I was tilted back as we headed upward. It felt like forever. It didn't help that the further up we went, the steeper the hill became. I wasn't ready. I was scared. I was an emotional wreck. One minute I was excited, and the next minute I was crying. Despite the emotional rollercoaster, I did it and I made it. It was time for the next adventure.

What was the name of the roller coaster you ask? Oh, it was called "The Dirty 30." Metaphorically speaking, that's exactly how I felt leading up to the day I officially turned thirty years old.

_____

> **"Note to self: Stop trying to figure out who everyone else wants you to be, and instead be who God designed and wants you to be"**

_____

I don't know if it was just me, but I dreaded turning thirty for a long time. The whole year leading up to my thirtieth birthday, I found myself struggling. I felt like I wasn't as accomplished as others or didn't have everything I was supposed to have by the age of thirty. Even though I was actually married by then, I still felt like I wasn't where I was supposed to be in terms of family, career, and other statuses that society tends to assign to women.

There's something about turning thirty. It's like a switch goes off and forces you to overanalyze the progress, or lack thereof, of your life especially when it comes to love and relationships. Thankfully, when I actually reached thirty, I felt much better about it. I focused on what I did have instead of what I didn't have.

As I reflect back to my childhood, I remember when I used to dream about meeting my Prince Charming, going on tour, and dancing my life away with Janet Jackson and Aaliyah (God rest her soul), or working in the entertainment business. I honestly remember dreaming more about my career goals than anything, but that didn't stop me from thinking I would be like Cinderella and find my Prince Charming.

Of course as I got older, it wasn't just Disney that sold the fairy tale or encouraged me to believe in happily ever after. Some of my favorite movies like Love Jones, The Best Man, and even Brown Sugar gave me hope of everlasting love or at least showed the struggles that come along with it. And as much as I loved those movies (and still do), I had to be honest with myself during my single season and remind myself that, no matter how great the movie, it was just that—a movie.

I often hear women state—and I used to proclaim myself—that they will be married by the age of twenty-five and have children by the age of thirty, so on and so forth. I had it all planned out, so I thought. But life happens and things don't always go as planned, especially if they don't necessarily fit with God's plans.

Furthermore, the older I got, the more I realized how unprepared I would have been had I received the things I prayed for when I prayed for them. Real life is quite different from make believe and reality TV, no matter how close to real life they may appear. If we're not careful, then we risk falling into the timeline trap and cause our relationship status to steer our happiness.

Our femininity and womanhood shouldn't be defined by other people's opinions or judgment based on our relationship status, physical appearance, career status, or whether we're mothers. At the end of the day, you have to live the best life you can live for you.

When it came to relationships, I used to worry so much about when, where, and how it was going to happen and with whom, so much so, that I missed out on other things that I could have and should have been doing in my own life.

Corrie ten Boom said, "Worrying is carrying tomorrow's load with today's strength—carrying two days at once. It is moving into tomorrow ahead of time. Worrying doesn't empty tomorrow of its sorrow, it empties today of its strength." That's exactly what I was doing. Instead of focusing on the present, I was more concerned about the future. I put my energy into things that ultimately I had no control over. I was over thirty and worried.

Please understand a woman can be any age (20, 30, 40, 50, etc.) and still have the "over thirty and worried" mindset. She's the girl who is overly obsessed with trying to find a man, or constantly sad about not having one. She has tried numerous relationships, but has yet to end up with Mr. Right. She has lost hope and given up, because of the hurt and pain she's endured along the way. Hence, she finds herself desperate, settling, stuck, or overwhelmed and consumed with thoughts of defeat. We know her, we are like her, or we are her at one at one time or another.

It's no secret that our insecurities and obsessions with life's timeline have been brought on by society and those closest to us. There is great pressure to be and do what others think we should be doing.

Sometimes, our friends and loved ones will have us feeling over thirty and worried, not to mention what we see on social media. We notice engagement photos online and see relationship statuses and announcements updated on our timelines. We see the couples in the mall or at the grocery store. We attend weddings and even play the role of bridesmaid. And the same question comes up each and every time, "When will it happen for me?"

We compare our lives to everyone else's and worry, because we think we will never experience the same happiness and love. We assume, because everyone else is on the track toward marriage, that we should at least be headed down the same path. What we fail to understand, however, is that everyone has a different life path. What may be right for someone else at that moment may not be right for you.

.

At times we allow our friends' actions to dictate our actions, because we think we have to do what they do. If they are single, then we want to be single. If they are in a relationship, then we feel like we should be in a relationship. If they get married, then we feel like it should be our time to get married. God designs a tailor-fit plan for all of us. What may fit someone else's life may not fit yours.

We even use our biological clocks as an excuse to act over thirty and worried. Of course, it is natural to be concerned with having children at an older age because of the major health risks, but it still shouldn't cause us to rush into a relationship.

What we think is impossible, God can make possible. Heck, I'm in my mid-thirties and still haven't given birth to a child, but I trust in God. If that's what He has planned for me and my husband, then it will come to pass. In the meantime, I will continue to enjoy the life God has blessed me with.

Trust me, I used to be that over thirty and worried girl and I was still in my twenties. Part of the reason I started acting like that was because of my bad experiences with certain guys. If you're anything like me, you might have dated a plethora of of men that included the good guys, the bad guys, the down-low guys, the cheating guys, the lying guys, the "want to play games all of the time" guys, the "I'm not ready for marriage" guys. You get the idea. Over time, it becomes frustrating and causes you to consider giving up. Eventually, I learned how to embrace the beauty of my singleness and my life as a whole. My relationship status, while important, was not as big an issue or as important as other things that people were really going through.

I learned how to be okay with being single instead of constantly worrying about it. Instead of claiming I was lonely and depressed, I learned how to re-direct my thoughts and focus. If the worry of getting and keeping a man consumes our minds, then we make ourselves vulnerable to situations where we date married men, covet other women's men, or end up settling.

There were been times when I settled, merely because I was desperate, needy or impatient. Neediness causes us to feel as if we have to have a man regardless of who he is. Because we're sometimes impatient and feel like time is running out, we start thinking every man we choose is "the one."

Being over thirty and worried causes us to do things we wouldn't otherwise do. It causes some of us to give up on love, which in turn makes us oblivious to it, even when it could be standing right in front of our faces. It causes us to force unhealthy relationships or situations that add no true value to our lives. It causes us to harbor bitterness and anger which pushes others away and makes us less attractive.

My mom, who has never been married, is the epitome of how not to be that girl. What I love about her is that, even though she's single and she's been through a lot, she hasn't given up on love. She's learned how to be single and satisfied.

My mom wasn't the type of woman who just sat around desperately waiting or chasing after men. Her feisty and strong-willed personality helps with that. Still, after all those years, she could have chosen to be an old, bitter Betty. Instead, she's constantly on the go and lives life to the fullest, all while still managing to give of herself, time, and resources to help many others. Not only is she busy with her personal tasks, but her newfound boyfriend definitely helps keep her busy by taking her out all the time. Life is short. Take a lesson from her and learn how to live, love, and appreciate your life.

I understand it's easier said than done when you're single and have been for a long time. I used to have my days when I would feel lonely and cry myself to sleep, wondering if it would ever happen for me. I know you, too, will have some days when you want to cry about it and wallow in that pain forever. But you can't stay there.

Take your moment, but then dust yourself off and keep it moving. Focus on the blessings that you do have. If you know you have a pessimistic attitude, then ask for renewal of your mind. Change the way you think, and maybe you will see a change in your life.

I know it's hard. I can't tell anyone how to feel or what to feel, especially when you're dealing with hurt and pain. All I know is that I wasted a lot of time crying and complaining over things that happened to me a long time ago. I stayed in that same place and allowed the pain to keep me broken for a long time. We can't continue weeping and wailing about things from the past that we make ourselves unavailable to hear from God, and not ready to receive what He has for us.

Why would God send you a man if you're still weeping and wailing over the last one who broke your heart? Why would He give you more if you can't thank Him enough for what you have now? How can He propel you into the future when you're still crying and weeping over what happened in the past?

For me, it all came down to repositioning my mind and my attitude. Even though there were days when I was frustrated or tired of the same thing, I had to find a way to focus on what was important. One thing I know for certain is, as soon as I let go my feelings of despair, sadness, and bitterness, that was when my husband came along.

I used to be bitter and hold onto to things from my past relationships. I started blaming everyone else for every issue I had but eventually, I had to acknowledge I was choosing to hold onto the bondage of bitterness. I couldn't just blame my ex-boyfriends for the pain I endured, because there were times when I put way too much effort and energy into trying to breathe life into dead situations.

I took ownership of my life and declared I would no longer let the chains keep me bound. No longer would I limit my potential blessings. We can't keep asking God to move in our lives and bless us if we we're not willing to move.

My dear sister, you may be in a situation right now and struggling to get over your past lover, but you can release that chain! You don't have to continue carrying the dead weight. Whatever chains you are holding onto right now—ex-lover, fatherless home, sexual immorality, sexual molestation, divorce, obesity, low self-esteem, drugs, alcohol, failure, and any others—release those chains and move toward the destiny to which God has called you.

Part of releasing the chains means releasing control. As much as we try to control our lives, we have to remember that, ultimately, God is in control. Even though we make plans, sometimes our plans fail. God's plans prevail. We have to learn how to be content with the life God gives us and with the fruits of our labor. We may not always understand why things happen the way they do, but we must remember to trust that He knows what's best. There's a reason why he's doing what he's doing.

Over-thirty-and-worried girl, please don't think that when you get married all of your issues will suddenly and magically disappear. People assume that's what happens when you get married. Wrong. Marriage delivers a whole new set of issues and obstacles that you have to overcome.

You have to stop thinking your life would be perfect if only you had a man. If you're blessed with a wonderful life, then I'd say you have more than enough for which to be thankful.

Matthew reminds us to "…seek first His kingdom and His righteousness, and all these things will be given to you as well" (Matthew 6:33 NIV). I know what you may be thinking: "But Lord, I've been following you and doing what you asked me to do." I know it gets frustrating, but one thing's for sure: I'd rather wait for God's best than settle for less. We're more patient with the guys we date than we are with God.

I know it hurts sometimes to think about the past, or to think about the future and wonder if and when it's ever going to happen. It can be quite lonely and frustrating. It will make you want to give up on the whole idea of love or even life itself, because we're nurturers by nature.

As women, it's quite natural for us to yearn for love and desire to be a good woman to a good man. After you reach a certain age and find it hard to even consider someone as a potential mate, it can be very draining on the heart and soul.

Hear me when I say this: There is no amount of hurt or heartache too big that God cannot heal. What others break, God can build back up. People may hurt us, but God can heal us. Trust God with your heart and your life.

Lesson Ten

Nothing happens overnight; things take time.

"She's engaged!"

It was the evening of Valentine's Day when the text message came through my phone.

I was so excited that I almost started crying when I heard the great news. I texted her immediately to congratulate her. I informed her that it was going to be one of the craziest, busiest, and best times of her life—wedding planning as a bride-to-be.

She told me people were already asking her about wedding dates, colors, the honeymoon, and everything. I calmly reminded her to enjoy the moment and first get used to having a ring on that ring finger.

What was so significant about this particular engagement wasn't the fact that she was getting married. It was the simple fact that this wonderful woman wasn't necessarily a friend of mine. She wasn't a former classmate or someone I recently met. She was actually one of my mom's closest friends and like an aunt to me. She was getting married for the very first time!

She was at an age (mid-fifties) when most people would have assumed it was too late or that it was never going to happen. This mother of one and the grandmother of four was going to add "wife" to her list of titles.

Just a few days or weeks later, she attended a bridal show, not as the mother of the bride, but this time as the bride. This time the celebration was for her. They say you shouldn't give up on love. Her story and her testimony of experiencing true love were living proof of that.

> "Note to self: The moment we stop worrying and looking is usually the very moment when it happens."

It's interesting that we are so quick to give up on love, or anything for that matter, when things don't go our way or when they don't happen when we want them to. But God's timetable isn't the same as ours.

My mom's friend's story—and that of many others—is inspiring, because I'm sure there were days throughout her life when she wondered, "Will I ever get married?" I'm sure she had plenty of days during certain seasons of her life when she thought it was never going to happen; however, she never gave up and, more importantly and just like my mom, she never stopped living her life. I know, because they've traveled and done quite a bit together.

Through this experience as well as my very own, I have determined that the moment we stop worrying and looking is usually the very moment when it happens or comes to us.

I can recall when I first moved to Atlanta. I was single and ready to mingle. I was in a new city and ready to live it up. For once, I was actually content with being single and had been for at least a year or so prior to meeting Eric. So, on a beautiful warm night, I was at a club enjoying life and having fun with my girls. While I took a break out on the patio to catch my breath (Lord knows I loved to cut a rug on the dance floor), I made eye contact with this handsome man. He started making his way toward me through the crowd. It was like a scene from a movie in which you see the story's hero coming toward the heroine very slowly. We conversed for a bit, exchanged numbers, and went our separate ways for the night.

A few days later, he called me. Then a few weeks later, we started dating and spending time together. We only got to hang out for roughly a month or so before it was time for him to head back to graduate school in Ohio.

Then, surprisingly, right before he left for school, he asked me to be his girl. Little did he know, I wasn't the least bit interested in pursuing a relationship. I remember vividly the conversation we had—and he does too—when I told him I was fine with being in the gray area. But he was not interested in the gray area. He knew what he wanted and he wasn't leaving until I agreed to give it a try. Although I was more interested in enjoying the city and having a good time as a single woman, obviously God had a different plan.

Fast forward to approximately a year and a few months later.

I had just gotten home from work. Eric called and asked me to accompany him and some colleagues from his job to dinner. However, I was exhausted and just didn't feel like going out. Even though he knew how tired I was, he wanted me to go because, apparently, his colleague's wife was going to be there as well.

Quite frankly, I wasn't in the mood. I had just walked through the door and was looking forward to putting on my pajamas and relaxing for the rest of the night. But he insisted I come with him and promised he would make it up to me. He wanted to make a good impression. Eventually, I gave in.

He said he would be by to pick me up within the hour. I hurried to my closet, put on a cute little dress, did something quick to my hair, applied a little eye shadow and lip gloss, and waited for him to arrive. When he picked me up, he looked very dapper and smelled great. I guess this was a big deal for him, but something seemed a little odd. He was acting a little different than usual, but I couldn't quite tell what it was.

While in the car, he blasted some song and sang like he was onstage performing. That part wasn't that odd, because he liked to warm up his vocals in the car. I was so tired that I just ignored it and started thinking about how long it would be before I could go back home and relax. After about thirty minutes, we arrived at an elegant steakhouse. The hostesses appeared to have already been waiting for us, because they said his last name when we arrived. I didn't really think anything of it, because I wanted to go home and go to sleep.

The hostess escorted us to our table and Eric pulled out my chair as usual. I noticed the other couple was missing. I asked him where the rest of the party was; he said his colleague had just texted him to say they were going to be late. We continued on without them and ordered drinks while we waited. Roughly 20 minutes or so passed, but there was still no sign of the other couple. I asked him again if he had heard from them. He told me they weren't coming.

Now, I was really confused and on the brink of catching an attitude, because the main reason I showed up to this dinner was because we were supposed to meet his colleagues there. But before I could even finish my thought and before I could even turn the situation into something it wasn't, Eric went down on one knee with a ring in his hand and proposed to me.

I was in shock, so much so that I couldn't really remember what all he said while he was down on one knee. I can't even recall how he got down there so fast. I guess I took too long to respond, because someone from across the room finally yelled, "Say yes! Say yes!"

Say yes?! Say yes to what? I was totally caught off-guard. I couldn't believe it was happening. I remember staring at the ring. It is rare for me to be at a loss of words, but this time I was because I was so astonished. I finally came back to my senses and exclaimed, "Yes!"

Eric put the ring on my finger and stood so we could embrace one another. Everyone clapped. I was engaged.

Immediately, tears started streaming down my face. There was so much excitement going on that we didn't even finish our food. We actually ended up giving it to a homeless person on the street when we left the restaurant. Then we headed to one of the places he took me to when we first started dating and topped off the night with some yummy dessert.

I'll never forget that night. It was surreal and totally unexpected. The same man I met at a club a year ago, the man I almost didn't give a chance to because I didn't want a long-distance relationship, the man I thought I didn't want to be with at first—that man was now the love of my life. It's funny how we think we know what we want, but God knows just what we need when we need it.

I remember walking down the aisle at our wedding and seeing that same man I met two years prior standing there and waiting for me. Up until that moment, I had been waiting for him to come along and now he was standing there waiting for me. As part of my personal vows, I told him: "...There was a time when, for a moment, I had given up on believing that I could ever experience true love in this lifetime. Then you came along and I could see God's love shining through you…"

True enough, there was a time when I gave up on love and marriage. People see our marriage today and assume it was all roses and rainbows for me. I didn't go from being single to being married overnight. It's obvious, just reading some of the stories in some of the earlier chapters, just how much I went through and the types of situations I endured during my single season. I went from parched to what Beyonce likes to refer to as "drunk in love." Eric didn't just fall into my lap.

Eric and I had struggles and obstacles when we started dating and even after we got married. Even though we were madly in love, that didn't exclude us from the tests and trials that everyone goes through in life. When we first started dating, there were things we had to deal with as it related to his ex-girlfriends, my ex-boyfriends, long distance, and trust. We definitely didn't deal with the kind of drama we were used to dealing with in the past, but we still had growing pains.

Marriage has a way of making you look at and learn more about yourself than you ever did before. It's like looking into a mirror, because there is always someone there to look back at you. That person will either reflect your image onto him or herself, or he or she will tell you about yourself. If you're not ready to be honest with yourself and not willing to compromise, then you're probably not ready for marriage…and that's okay.

During our first year of marriage, we went through many ups and downs. We used to have big arguments over the smallest things. We had to learn how to live together and be around each other all the time. We had to learn each others' habits, nuances, and pet peeves.

I'll never forget a big fight we had over what was later just a misunderstanding. It got pretty heated and the timing could not have been any worse, because my mother and some of her friends were on their way to visit us. Because I wear my emotions on my sleeves, I had to tell my mom we were dealing with a situation, but I didn't go into too much detail.

Nothing against my mom, but I learned early that you can't always to tell everyone about your problems. It paints a negative picture in other people's minds. Even when you and your spouse have moved on, it may take your family and friends longer to get over it and cause them to hold a grudge.

Nevertheless, I knew we weren't going to be all "lovey-dovey" with each other, so I just told her we were having a little spat so she wouldn't suspect it was something much more serious. A few days passed during which I ignored him or spoke to him as little as possible (not that I suggest that method). Eventually, we had a counselor or marriage mentors come over. They helped us work through the disagreement.

Although we worked it all out, it drained us mentally and emotionally. We learned that ignoring each other and walking away wasn't the best way to resolve an issue. Each year, our relationship gets better and better. Now, it's highly unlikely for us to go long, if at all, without speaking. We still have our disagreements, as most normal couples do, but we're able to move on much faster.

The point of it all is to understand that things take time. We can't assume after one date that a certain guy is going to be our husband. We can't assume that marriage is going to solve all our problems. We can't assume everything is going to be peachy if and when marriage does happen. Just like it took time for me to meet my husband, it has taken time for us to get to where we are within our marriage. There is a reason for the process. Most times the reason isn't about the wait; rather, it's about what we do while we're waiting.

Just recently, we talked about the story of Abraham and Sarah in one of our marriage classes. For those of you who aren't familiar with the story, Abraham and Sarah were married, but Sarah was barren. God promised Sarah and Abraham that she would give birth to a child, not just any child but the future leader of nations, Isaac. Sarah got a little tired of waiting on God, so she convinced her husband to sleep with her maidservant, Hagar. Abraham acquiesced and Hagar bore a son.

Then just as God promised, Sarah, in her old age, became pregnant. The only problem was that she now she had to deal with the consequences of her previous decision to go against what God told her to do. Instead of waiting for God to deliver her baby, she took it upon herself to change the plan. So, she had to figure out what to do about the other son.

One might think Sarah would have been fine with the Hagar situation, considering she was the mastermind behind the whole thing; but, once she considered the possibility that Hagar's son could inherit more than her own son, Isaac, the tables turned. She sent Hagar and her son away, but God still blessed them.

Talk about some baby mama drama.

It was at that moment when I think Sarah, like many of us, realized she trusted herself more than she trusted God. She prayed for something, but didn't believe it was going to happen. God told her it would come to pass, but she tried to make it happen in her own way and in her own time.

I've been like Sarah—not that I've borne a child—in that I've created messy situations trying to do what I wanted to do versus what God wanted me to do. Some of us constantly pray and wait for something we may not be quite ready for. We have to be mindful of that which we pray and ask God for.

I prayed a lot of prayers and ignored a few, because I was more concerned with what I wanted versus what I needed. At times, I've had to ask God for a "will alignment"—that's when you make sure your plans are lined up with God's plans for your life.

If God has promised us something, we have to trust and believe that it will come to pass, even if that means waiting longer than we expected. I truly believe God wants to see just how much we trust Him without the things we pray for, so He knows we'll still trust Him even after He provides what we pray for. The waiting period can be long and weary, but it's also the best time for us to prove our faith to God and for God to help perfect it.

One thing about love…you can't rush it. It should come naturally. Even though the process may take a little longer, remember what God has for you is for you. If it's in His will for your life—whether married, single, dating or whatever—it will come to pass.

We have to do like T. D. Jakes tells us and keep pushing. I remember reading one of his first books in which he used the analogy of childbirth to describe the pain and suffering we often endure as a result of broken relationships, heartache, and hardships. I have never experienced childbirth, but, from what I hear, it is one of the most painful experiences known. Still, it is one of the most beautiful and awe-inspiring events one will experience in life.

There are times when mothers must endure excruciating pain during delivery. For most, the pain can linger after the baby is born and the woman must take time to heal before she can return to normal activities.

Prior to Eric, I went through some pain. I went through heartache and betrayal. Prior to Eric, I had to take time alone for myself so I could properly heal, but it was all for my good. I couldn't see it then—Lord knows I didn't want to see it then—because all I wanted was the delivery but without having to endure some labor pains along the way. I wanted my "Prince Charming," but I didn't want to have to kiss a few frogs along the way. I wanted to be with the right man, but I wasn't willing to work on being the right woman. I was tired of waiting and wanted what I wanted when I wanted it. But God had a plan for me.

Just like a woman has to endure contractions and keep pushing, we, too, must keep pushing. Who knew God had a special delivery waiting for me around the corner? Had I stayed weeping and wailing and focused on the past, I might have missed my future blessing.

I know it's easy to give up because it feels like it's been forever, but now is not the time to stop pushing. Just because it looks like God isn't moving in one area of your life doesn't mean He can't move in other areas of your life. So, keep pushing no matter what.

Just like the arrival of a newborn baby, there is something about the arrival of true love that makes it worthwhile. Understand, however, that although newborns and new relationships can bring you joy and happiness, they are not the ultimate source of your joy. God is the ultimate source of our joy. He can give you hope and reassure you that you will be blessed with or without a husband.

His joy will allow you to smile and feel renewed, even when you walk through the mall and see your ex-boyfriend with his new girlfriend. His joy will make you smile and be polite and cordial. His joy will remind you that God cherishes every single thing about you, even when your ex-boyfriend continuously ignores you and acts as if you never meant anything to him. His joy and peace can help you get through those tough nights when you're home alone with no one to hold. He can help you feel content with whatever your status may be.

Every struggle I endured has developed my strength. Every situation that hurt me has taught me how to heal and help others. They say good things come to those who wait; anything worth having in life is worth the wait. Plus, the delay makes you even more appreciative because of how long you may have had to wait.

Whether it's a new career, a new car, a new business, or a new man, you may have to endure some pain and suffering along the way. But the pain will only last for a season. If you are enduring pain even as you read this book thinking about your failed relationship and how he doesn't love you anymore, know that your pain won't last forever.

Things were different when I met my husband; there was a past before my present. There were frogs before my prince. I made mistakes before I made better decisions. There was pain before my pleasure. There was heartache before my happiness. There was rejection before acceptance. There was a time when I felt "parched" when it came to love and relationships. Just like someone who is desperate for a drink, I was desperate for a man's love.

I yearned for love, but I was doing all the wrong things to get it and the guys were doing all the wrong things to prove they "loved" me. The lack of solid prospects also lengthened my wait, which I'm sure some of my single sisters fully understand. Plain and simple, my love fountain was dry.

Eventually, I pulled myself together and learned how to be single and content with that. How, you ask? I just reached a point where I was sick and tired of being sick and tired. I was fed up with being fed up. I was tired of always being the one doing everything. I was tired of waiting for him to come around. I was tired of hearing the excuses as to why two people who were supposedly in love could not be together. I was tired of waiting, tired of crying, and tired of staying in the same place while he moved on with his life. I was tired of constantly thinking about him or dwelling on the relationship.

It was time that I renewed my mind. I was finally ready to focus on things that would bring life and happiness, not heartache or sadness. If only we could move on as easily as some others do after a relationship has ended. Nevertheless, it definitely didn't happen overnight.

I took some much needed time and learned how to be by myself. I learned how to have fun, relax, and enjoy life more. I started reading and meditating and hanging out with my friends. I started putting me first. If I had been able to afford it, I would have traveled a lot more. I learned how to let it flow and let it go. I decided I wouldn't focus all of my attention on my relationship status.

All of that helped me, because that was also around the time when I packed up my stuff and moved to Atlanta. Sometimes a change of location helps to change our perspective and that's exactly what I needed. It may sound cliché, but I let go and let God take control, because I knew if He wanted me to be with someone then He would make it happen. After moving to Atlanta, the rest was history.

When my husband came along, it was like I experienced a blackout. New memories replaced old ones and made it that much easier to forget about ex-boyfriends and the constant drama. Even though the effects of past hurt and pain lingered at times, the bitterness and anger slowly started to fade. Eventually, I was strong enough to wave goodbye to the past and greet the future.

My husband brings about the balance I need and helps hold me up, especially when life gets hectic or I feel unsteady. He's the ying to my yang. We help each other grow. When I'm weak, he's strong (and vice versa). Even though our overall personalities differ, that difference helps balance us both. I can be the loud and boisterous one, while he tends to take on the calmer and cooler role. Some days we switch, but everything still balances out in the end.

There's nothing like waking up next to my man without feeling regret. I'm blessed and content knowing that I'm with the person God intended for me.

I say all of this not only to share how great love can be, but to encourage someone else who may feel how I used to feel – parched and desperately seeking or waiting for something real. If it can happen for me and if it's God's will for your life, then it can happen for you. Just understand that nothing happens overnight. Things take time to develop.

We live in a world where we want instant gratification and everything seems to happen immediately. Remember when we had to wait days before we could get our pictures developed?

.

Remember when we had no choice but to mail letters and cards, because we didn't have access to email or the internet? Remember there was a time when we didn't even have the option of meeting someone online? Technology has changed and time will make you feel like you're not moving fast enough when it comes to dating, love, and relationships.

Be reminded that God is neither limited by time nor age. I know couples who have been together since they were teenagers and I know more seasoned couples who are experiencing true love and marriage for the first time in their fifties and beyond.

Everything happens when it's supposed to happen and when we're ready for it to happen. I didn't experience true love until God knew I was ready. Even though there were times when I thought I was ready, I wasn't. Everything I experienced leading up to my husband made me even that much more appreciative and grateful for the love I have now.

We can't get so caught up in the why—Why me? Why hasn't it happened for me yet?—so much so that we miss the what: What is the purpose? What does God want me to glean from this? What can I do to show Him I trust Him?

It's hard when we can't see God's next move for our lives or when we don't have all the answers. But, if we didn't have to rely on or fully trust Him, then what would be the purpose of our faith?

Everything that did or didn't happen, every door that closed; everyone who left; everyone who stayed; every relationship that started or ended; and, every broken heart you endured has prepared you in some way or another for where you are right now in your life. Trust God and trust the process.

Romans 8:28 NIV reminds us, "And we know that in all things God works for the good of those who love him, who have been called according to his purpose." May you be encouraged through my experiences and through God's word and believe that He is working for your good. You must be able to look at yourself in the mirror and say, "I'm good," no matter what my relationship status may be.

Acknowledgements:

For my Heavenly Father who speaks through me,

For my wonderful husband—he is the constant in my life, and he sacrifices so much so that I can walk the path that God has laid out for me,

For my mother—she always encourages me and I am the woman I am today because of her,

For every friend or family member I called, texted, emailed repeatedly to ask for their opinion about the book cover, the content, the title, etc.,

For every person who has read, shared or commented on any of my blog articles,

For every person that has sincerely prayed for me or encouraged me in some way,

For all of the support,

I sincerely thank God for you and I appreciate you more than you know!

Made in United States
North Haven, CT
01 December 2022

27658927R00093